ON THE BUS

(TOP LEFT) PRANKSTER GEORGE WALKER
WITH HIS HAND-PAINTED LOTUS SPORTS
CAR. (RON BEVIRT)

(TOP RIGHT) BEAT LEGEND AND MAIN
DRIVER NEAL CASSADY IN WIKIEUP,
ARIZONA, AN EARLY STOP ON THE
ORIGINAL BUS TRIP. PRANKSTER STEVE
LAMBRECHT RECALLS: "THEY HAD SPRAYED
MY SHIRT AND MADE ME PUT IT ON AND I
GOT PAINT ALL OVER MY BACK. [THEN] I
REMEMBER NEAL TRYING TO PLAY THE
GUITAR AND I THOUGHT, 'HE CAN'T PLAY
THE GUITAR, WHAT IS HE DOING?'"
(RON BEVIRT)

(BOTTOM) KEN KESEY AT THE ACID TEST
GRADUATION, ON HALLOWEEN NIGHT, 1966,
IN SAN FRANCISCO. (TED STRESHINSKY)

(TOP) GRETCHEN FETCHIN OUTSIDE OF THE BUS IN LARRY MCMURTRY'S YARD IN HOUSTON, A STOP ON THE PRANKSTERS' ORIGINAL TRIP. (RON BEVIRT)

(BOTTOM LEFT) KEN KESEY IN TEXAS. KESEY SAID IN A 1967 PACIFICA RADIO INTERVIEW: "EVERY TIME YOU TRY TO LAY YOUR HANDS ON SOMETHING AND GET HOLD OF IT . . . YOU'VE SOLD YOURSELF DOWN THE RIVER. IT'S A LIE. THE FIRST PRANKSTER RULE IS THAT NOTHING LASTS. AND IF YOU START THERE, AND REALLY BELIEVE THAT NOTHING LASTS, YOU TRY TO ACHIEVE NOTHING AT ALL TIMES . . . " (RON BEVIRT)

(BOTTOM RIGHT) FIVE MEMBERS OF THE GRATEFUL DEAD ON THE STEPS OF THEIR HOME AT 710 ASHBURY STREET, IN A PHOTO ORIGINALLY SHOT FOR A 1966 NEWSWEEK STORY ON THE "SAN FRANCISCO RENAISSANCE." (GENE ANTHONY)

"FURTHUR" BEING PREPARED FOR THE ACID TEST GRADUATION. (TED STRESHINSKY)

(ABOVE) THE BUS AT SAN FRANCISCO STATE UNIVERSITY FOR THE "WHAT'S HAPPENING"
FESTIVAL. PAUL KRASSNER: "THE BUS WAS HARD TO MISS WHEN IT CAME THROUGH YOUR
TOWN . . . AND SO IT TURNED PEOPLE ON, OR EVEN IF IT TURNED PEOPLE OFF, THEY STILL
RESPONDED TO IT." (GENE ANTHONY)

(RIGHT) KEN KESEY AS "CAPTAIN FLAG." (RON BEVIRT)

THE BUS AT THE LOVE PAGEANT RALLY. MEMBERS OF THE JEFFERSON AIRPLANE AND THE GRATEFUL DEAD ARE AMONG THOSE ON THE ROOF. (GENE ANTHONY)

On The Bus

The Complete Guide to the Legendary Trip of Ken Kesey and the Merry Pranksters and the Birth of the Counterculture

BY PAUL PERRY

"Flashbacks"

BY KEN "THE INTREPID TRAVELLER" BABBS

Featuring photos by Ron "Hassler" Bevirt, Allen Ginsberg, Gene Anthony, Ted Streshinsky, and Others

Forewords by Hunter S. Thompson and Jerry Garcia

Edited by Michael Schwartz and Neil Ortenberg

Plexus, London

Published by Plexus Publishing Limited
26 Dafforne Road
London SW17 8TZ
First printing 1991

Perry, Paul
 On the bus: the complete guide to the legendary trip of
Ken Kesey and the Merry Pranksters and the birth of the
counterculture.
 1. United States, Young persons, Subcultures, history
I. Title II. Babbs, Ken
306.1

 ISBN 0-85965-196-7

Published by arrangement with Thunder's Mouth Press

Book design and composition by the Sarabande Press
Printed in Great Britain

For my son Paul,
who is definitely on the bus.

NEAL CASSADY IN A SCENE FROM THE PRANKSTERS' FILM, *THE MERRY PRANKSTERS SEARCH FOR THE COOL PLACE*, THE RESULT OF NEARLY UNLIMITED FILMING, WITH TWO CAMERAS, IN AN ATTEMPT TO DOCUMENT THE PRANKSTERS' TRIP AND CAPTURE REALITY IN ALL ITS UNEDITED COMPLEXITY.

Contents

FOREWORDS

"There were no rules, fear was unknown, and sleep was out of the
question. . . ."   *by Hunter S. Thompson*   xv

Behind the Wheel with Neal   *by Jerry Garcia*   xvii

EDITORS' PREFACE   xix

AUTHOR'S ACKNOWLEDGEMENTS   xxiii

FROM *The Electric Kool-Aid Acid Test*   *by Tom Wolfe*   xxv

PART I: ORIGINS   1

The father of LSD & his problem child . . . the first Captain Trips meets Aldous
Huxley & they see "nothing but the truth" . . . Henry Luce sees God on the golf
course . . . Leary + mushrooms = magic . . . CIA + LSD = MK-ULTRA . . . the
psychedelic Left Bank of Palo Alto . . . "the equivalent to any literary scene" . . .
Perry Lane's bohemia . . . Stanford + acid + mental hospital = *One Flew Over
the Cuckoo's Nest* . . . "as big as a man feels it's in him to be."

PART II: THE TRIP   41

The Intrepid Traveller's version of the trip . . . mysticism & merriment in a mud
hole near Wikieup . . . Stark Naked earns her name at Larry McMurtry's home
. . . the hits just keep on coming . . . The Beats meet the Pranksters . . . on to
Millbrook . . . a meeting of the acid tribes . . . "I'm not sure why they came"—
Leary . . . go West young men, go West . . . Better living through chemistry.

PART III: THE ACID TESTS—AND BEYOND   109

Home to La Honda . . . "no left turn unstoned" . . . the tribe grows & glows . . . the
reel story: a 45-hour movie . . . the Hell's Angels take acid, party, & go up in
flames . . . "I thought they would take the Pranksters apart like cooked
chicken"—Hunter S. Thompson . . . someone pops the question: "Can *you* pass
the Acid Test?" . . . astronauts of inner space—thousands of them . . . Kesey
tweaks the tail of the law . . . "I think he tried to get arrested" . . . Kesey "hides
out" in Mexico with a bus load of Pranksters at "La Casa Purina" . . . "Everybody
was very paranoid"—Robert Stone . . . back over the border disguised as a
singing cowboy . . . busted in grand style . . . back home to the farm.

PART IV: AFTERMATH   183

Where are they now? . . . tributes to Neal Cassady.

EDITORS' EPILOGUE   191

A FINAL WORD   195

"There were no rules, fear was unknown, and sleep was out of the question. . . ."

BY HUNTER S. THOMPSON

Twenty-five years ago. That's incredible. It seems like at the most twenty-five months. It was a wild time, folks—the good old days for sure. We stomped on the terra. San Francisco in 1965 was the best place in the world to be. Anything was possible. The crazies were seizing the reins, craziness hummed in the air, and the heavyweight king of the crazies was a rustic boy from La Honda named Ken Kesey.

He had the craziest gang in the West. LSD-25 was legal in those days, and Kesey's people were seriously whooping it up. It was a whole new world. "Do it *now*" was the motto, and anything not naked was wrong. The best minds of our generation somehow converged on La Honda, and Kesey had room for them all. His hillside ranch in the canyon became the world capital of madness. There were no rules, fear was unknown, and sleep was out of the question.

How I became involved with these people is a long queer story: I'd done an article on the Hell's Angels for *The Nation*, and once that was out I had my entree. After that, as far as the Angels were concerned, I was "good people."

As for Kesey, I always liked his work and believed then, as I still do, that he is one of the really good writers of our time. Also, I'd been to one of the Prankster gatherings at Kesey's La Honda place and I liked it.

So I happened to have a foot in both camps, and what I did, basically, was act as a social director mixing a little Hell's Angel with a little Prankster to see what you came up with—for fun, of course, but I was also acting in my own interest because I wanted to have something interesting to write about. To do this safely, well, you got to have control; my control ran out early on.

To the credit of Kesey and the Pranksters, they were too crazy to be scared. Kesey invited the boys down to La Honda for a full scale set-to, with scores of Angels converging for rapine, LSD, and fried chicken. I told Kesey that he would deserve to be shot as a war criminal if he went through with this. I remember thinking, "What the fuck have I wrought here? I have destroyed all kinds of things I've been entrusted to at least be careful with." I was opposed, but there wasn't time to be opposed, there was only time to turn on my tape recorder.

I remember the hordes snarling down the road and amassing near the big welcome banner the Pranksters had stretched across the gate. At the entrance stood the young innocents, eager to extend their tribal hospitality.

It was quite a scene. People were bursting into flame everywhere you looked. There were speakers everywhere—all around the trees—and there were other big delay speakers out on the cliff with their wires strung across the road. And there were about six cop cars parked in the road, flashing lights, cops everywhere, they could see right across the creek. And all the while more Angels were coming down the road and being welcomed with great happiness and friendliness. The simple fact that carnage was averted was impressive; but this was incredible.

Yep. That was Uncle Ken. He couldn't laugh unless he was going fast, and then you couldn't hear him at all because the wind made his lips flap like rubber.

One thing he never knew, though, was what it felt like to get from his house back to mine in 33 minutes on a 650 BSA Lightning. . . . It was 55 miles—which is very, very fast. But there was no speed limit on Highway One back then, and on most nights there was no traffic. All you had to do was screw it all the way over and hang on. Everything after that was like being shot through the looking glass. It was faster than a brain full of DMT—one of the most powerful psychedelics ever made. As Grace Slick observed one day, "Acid is like being sucked up a tube, but DMT is like being shot out of a cannon."

Maybe I have gone faster, since then, but somehow it's always felt slow.

Behind the Wheel with Neal

BY JERRY GARCIA

Cassady did something that changed my life. It was after the Acid Test in Watts. George Walker was parking the bus and Cassady was too messed up to drive. He'd been on the road all night, driving back from San Francisco, trying to make it to the Acid Test, and didn't get there until it was nearly over and we were packing up and leaving.

That was the night everybody was terribly overdosed. Neal must have caught up fast. By dawn he didn't have his shirt on. No shoes. Just those shapeless gray pants. And for some reason he wasn't speaking. Sometimes he'd get to that place where he was beyond speaking. Even without talking Cassady was completely there. He was motioning George into a parking place. We were at Wavy Gravy's and the parking place was just opposite the house. There was George leaning out the window of the bus and Neal in back of him giving him signals, a little to the left, a little to the right, all with gestures. Neal directed him right into a stop sign and the bus knocked it over and shaved it clean off.

Neal immediately picked it up and tried to stick it back in the hole. And down the street here came two little old ladies on their way to church. Meanwhile Neal's walking away from the sign real fast, and it hung for a minute and started to topple, and just before it fell and hit the ground he caught it and put it back up. Then the ladies see him: Is it a disreputable drunk or what? He isn't talking, but he decides to clean up his act, and what he does is try to hide the stop sign behind him until the ladies pass by. It was like an elegant, physical, Buster Keaton ballet. There was no point to it and it wasn't a verbal experience. It just ended, and it represents the way he moved through space. Effortless and perfect. And not divorced from the old ladies, either. He took them into account.

I hit him for a ride back to our house, and it was just me and him for some reason in that old brown Ford sedan we used for a gopher car. And of course, Neal was driving, and it was very strange because most of the time when you got behind the wheel with Neal it was like an adventure; but this time we left the place and pulled out onto the street and drove at a speed of maybe eight, twelve miles an hour, and kept going at that speed without either of us saying a word about. He'd look over at me every once in a while, and we were strangely close. And that was it. Hard to explain now, but it was right-on at the time. That burned-out feeling after a night on acid. Him behind the wheel in an exceptional state. There was nobody out, the streets were bare, and when you don't have to talk to the person next to you, that's real clean. Takes a certain thing not to try to keep anything up, not to have to entertain one another.

He was the mellow Neal, just a guy, just like us. But there was a mysterious thing there, too. I had the feeling that I was involved in a lesson. . . .

Neal represented a model to me of how far you could take it in the individual way, in the sense that you weren't going to *have* a work, you were going to *be* the work. Work in real time, which is a lot like a musician's work.

I was oscillating at the time. I had originally been an art student and was wavering between one-man-one-work or being involved in something that was dynamic and ongoing and didn't necessarily stay any one way—and, also, something in which you weren't the only contributing factor.

I decided to go with what was dynamic and with what more than one mind was involved with.

The decision I came to was to be involved in a group thing, namely the Grateful Dead, and I'm still involved in it.

Editors' Preface

In the 1960s, Ken Kesey and the Merry Pranksters were among the most visible and colorful leaders of what is now known, for the sake of convenience, as the "counterculture." Though a useful label, it gives the impression of a period now dead and gone.

Is this counterculture a movement limited to the history of the 1960s? Paul Krassner, social satirist and editor of *The Realist*, doesn't think so.

"I think that there's always been a counterculture," he said, recently. "In cave-dwelling times, when they were writing some official version of things on cave walls, I'm sure there was some kid writing some alternative on another boulder out in the fields, and that was the first underground press. There's always been some element of society that says, 'Hey, wait a minute, the priorities of civilization are insane and we don't have to accept them.'"

And yet the counterculture which existed in the 1960s was extraordinary. Its uniqueness resulted from the unprecedented position of the American empire: From 1945, the U.S. was a society with near-total military and economic dominance of the world, with a gigantic, adequately fed, comfortable, educated middle class, and a demographic surge of kids accustomed to food, housing, clothing, and health as a birthright. For perhaps the first time, most of the people in a society found their primary needs of survival met, freeing them to seek pleasure instead of simply struggling for survival.

Also, as Timothy Leary told Paul Perry, technological developments helped create an environment where a psychedelic counterculture was possible. "I think that all these things [were] pretty historically inevitable, when you had modern technology producing psychedelic drugs mass-market and then you had electronic amplification [recording and broadcast] of sound."

Though technology would make it possible for individuals to experience the world in a new way, it had previously led the way to a narrowing of the publicly discussed possibilities of thought and individual experience. During what is now called the "Eisenhower Era," government, business, and mass communications tightened standards of acceptable political orthodoxy in public schooling, higher education, books and magazines, entertainment, and culture. Enormous tensions built up. By the 1960s, the possibilities for individual freedom were greater than ever, yet public culture was sterile. Material abundance was commonplace, but every city had slums and the country was at war. Young people started questioning, and seeing through, the contradictions of American life.

In 1960, the first wave of babies born to the families of returning World War II veterans were becoming teenagers. By 1970, the effects of some kind of youth-led rebellion had been felt in the United States and beyond. There is no doubt that this rebellion left behind lasting effects—some profound and some trivial.

Among the most notable accomplishments: Youth-led opposition to the war in Vietnam, which (arguably) raised the costs of the war to the point where escalation was halted; challenges to institutions of education, government, family, and authority of all stripes; new forms of community, music, and personal appearance; and new attitudes toward sexuality, the natural world, spiritual exploration, and drug use.

When Ken Kesey and the Merry Pranksters took their bus ride in the summer of 1964, they served as a symbol of the changes underway, if not, in fact, as a signal for the counterculture to emerge. Either way, as advance publicity for the countercultural movement they succeeded beyond anyone's expectations—although Prankster Ken Babbs firmly asserts to this day that they had no such ambitions at the time. "The Pranksters didn't set out to turn anyone onto anything. We were making movies. We were using LSD to expand our consciousness. We were going to New York City for various reasons, mostly personal. And we became involved in ongoing work that is still ongoing."

Though Pranksters are leery of making grand claims about the significance of their activities, Paul Krassner, from his perspective as a fellow traveller, recognizes and appreciates the specific contributions that the Pranksters made in larger social movements of the time:

> I think that they were the most colorful and visible countercultural leaders—and I
> mean literally colorful and literally visible—because the bus was hard to miss when
> it came through your town. It was wildly painted and filled with sound equipment

and people with bizarre clothes. And so it turned people on, or even if it turned people off, they still responded to it.

While the Pranksters are known primarily for attracting attention, this is not to say that the act of attracting attention was itself unimportant. Journalist and social historian Lauren Kessler, who has written extensively about the counterculture of the 1960s, offered these thoughts in response to questions about the role the Pranksters played in these movements:

> The Merry Pranksters showed what was possible. They served as a trans-generational bridge between the Beats and hippies, and their contribution was greater than the sum of its parts. Yes, it involved acid rock music; yes, it was about staging a grand goof, about being yourself in the most outrageous way you'd care to be; yet it was something bigger.
>
> What was unique was that they were making a choice to have a good time 'in your face.'. . . In the context of the times it was an unusual and liberating thing to do.

In the process they were highly visible, but it's important to note that they were not the only vanguard figures of the psychedelic movement. There were groups in San Francisco such as the Diggers and Chet Helms's group, the Family Dog, as well as others throughout the country which were using group activity, hallucinogens, and spectacle to explore—to extend—the range of the thinkable, and to influence the public to question accepted values.

However, what helped put the Pranksters on the most visible front lines was probably the fact that they were a team with *two* major American literary celebrities (Ken Kesey and Neal Cassady), and that they helped organize now-legendary events that helped connect people in a movement that spread across the country.

In their time, the Pranksters were among the thousands in the first wave of people who took LSD, which included members of the Grateful Dead whose concerts have, in turn, initiated over a million people (by Timothy Leary's estimate). The fact that so many people have been willing to take acid has had some profound consequences. For many, the drug has allowed them to develop insights that enabled them to *deprogram* themselves from the culture they were born into. Lauren Kessler explains:

> LSD has a lot to do with removing systems of control—of seeing what's going to happen without knowing, of accepting the notion of throwing yourself into the void

and allowing the world to happen to you without the protective screening mechanisms we usually have. It is a drug that is revolutionary in the sense that it makes the mental barriers between sexes, races, or countries seem absurd.

Or, to put it a different way, Paul Krassner says that taking LSD "meant that people trusted their friends more than the government." It also meant trusting one's own judgment, instead of automatically deferring to authority.

Ken Babbs points out that the Pranksters' attempts to open perspectives did not depend solely on the use of LSD. Ultimately, LSD became just another of the tools they used to free individuals from perspectives which enslaved them. "We knew that not everyone was strong enough to get through tripping without suffering some kind of damage," Babbs said. "Our purpose was to use the drug to break up established patterns and, while in a heightened state of awareness, do our work as writers, musicians, rappers, cinematographers, social engineers, still photographers, and dramatists—and to record it while it was happening."

It was this exercise of freedom, in a way that encouraged questioning, which found expression in the anti-war movement, the ecology movement, a rich variety of people's rights movements, and a youth culture with its own mass events, like the "Be-ins" and Woodstock. The resultant youth culture also popularized paperbacks like *The Whole Earth Catalogue*, Robert A. Heinlein's *Stranger in a Strange Land*, Tom Wolfe's *The Electric Kool-Aid Acid Test* (a creative but essentially factual account of many of the events discussed in this book), and works by Hermann Hesse, Richard Brautigan, and Ken Kesey. Also worthy of mention is the probable influence that the Pranksters had on the Beatles "going psychedelic." Their album and film *Magical Mystery Tour*, which involved LSD-inspired adventures on a bus, might well have been influenced by accounts of the Pranksters' adventures.

But America has always had a counterculture and, though perhaps not as visible, it has one now; it was no aberration of the 1960s. It might be said that the counterculture of the sixties was an expression of the human spirit, reasserting itself and reemerging through the restrictive social conditioning of the modern world.

Paul Krassner, in fact, sees the Pranksters as representatives of a venerable American tradition. "They were truly followers of the American pioneer spirit," he said, "but without killing any Indians in the process."

—Michael Schwartz
Neil Ortenberg

Acknowledgements

In books, as in movies, the most visible participants (in this case, the writer) frequently gets the credit when many people do the work. To help prevent such an oversight here, I'd like to acknowledge the work of Neil Ortenberg, Thunder's Mouth Press's publisher and senior editor, and of editor Michael Schwartz, who slaved long and hard over this book. Both of these gentlemen are skilled diplomats as well as excellent editors.

Special thanks also go to Gurney Norman, who took great pains to present his Stanford days in vivid detail, as did Ed McClanahan and Robert Stone. Hunter S. Thompson was especially candid in his remembrances, talking one day from early morning until after sun-up about the time he spent among the Hell's Angels and the Merry Pranksters. Allen Ginsberg made rich contributions to this book, both in anecdotes and photographs. I also want to express my gratitude to Pranksters Ken Babbs, Ron Bevirt (whose photographs were one of the inspirations for this book), Steve Lambrecht, Denise Kaufmann, and Lee Quarnstrom for their generous contributions of time, insight, suggestions, and factual clarification. I'd also like to thank Timothy Leary, Baba Ram Dass, Gordon Lish, Lauren Kessler, and Paul Krassner for their invaluable participation, and William S. Burroughs and Lawrence Ferlinghetti for their graciousness in allowing us to reprint their reminiscences of Neal Cassady.

Additional thanks go to photographers Ted Streshinsky, Gene Anthony, Steve Dossey (whose valuable piece on Neal Cassady appears in the "Aftermath" section), Barbara Lish, and Ann Charters for use of their outstanding work, which allowed us to illustrate the post-bus trip period.

For help in obtaining crucial archival material, we thank Pam Allen and the *Times*

Tribune in Palo Alto, California, Karen Bartholomew of the Stanford University News Service, the Pacifica Radio Archive, and Jacqueline Gens and Bob Rosenthal, who work with Allen Ginsberg.

Also playing important roles in the development of this book in its final form were Jean Casella, Thunder's Mouth Press's managing editor; Russell "Rusty" Hoover, who offered a number of important suggestions; Brad Jacobson, whose internship at Thunder's Mouth Press proved to be a major support to this project; and Eugenie Gavenchack, whose legal advice and keen eye for potential hazards are very much appreciated.

Among the works which were especially helpful in compiling this book were *Acid Dreams: The CIA, LSD and the Sixties Rebellion*, by Martin A. Lee and Bruce Shlain, published by Grove Press; *Storming Heaven*, by Jay Stevens, from Atlantic Monthly Press; and *The Electric Kool-Aid Acid Test* by Tom Wolfe, originally published by Farrar, Straus and Giroux.

Finally, a special thanks to Ken Kesey, who remains the best.

—Paul Perry

From The Electric Kool-Aid Acid Test

BY TOM WOLFE

"I couldn't tell you for sure which of the Merry Pranksters got the idea for the bus, but it had the Babbs touch. It was a superprank, in any case. The original fantasy, here in the spring of 1964, had been that Kesey and four or five others would get a station wagon and drive to New York for the New York World's Fair. On the way they could shoot some film, make some tape, freak out on the Fair and see what happened. They would also be on hand, in New York, for the publication of Kesey's second novel, *Sometimes a Great Notion*, early in July. So went the original fantasy. . . ."

. . .

"Kesey gave the word and the Pranksters set upon it one afternoon. They started painting it and wiring it for sound and cutting a hole in the roof and fixing up the top of the bus so you could sit up there in the open air and play music, even a set of drums and electric guitars and electric bass and so forth, or just ride. Sandy [Lehmann-Haupt] went to work on the wiring and rigged up a system with which they could broadcast from inside the bus, with tapes or over microphones, and it would blast outside over powerful speakers on top of the bus. There were also microphones outside that would pick up sounds along the road and broadcast them inside the bus. There was also a sound system inside the bus so you could broadcast to one another over the roar of the engine and the road. You could also broadcast over a tape mechanism so that you said something, then heard your own voice a second later in variable lag and could rap off of that if you wanted to. Or you could put on earphones and rap simultaneously off sounds from outside, coming in one ear, and sounds from inside, your own sounds, coming in the other ear. There was going to be no goddamn sound on that whole trip, outside the bus, inside the bus, or inside your own freaking larynx, that you couldn't tune in on and rap off of.

"The painting job, meanwhile, with everybody pitching in in a frenzy of primary colors, yellows, oranges, blues, reds, was sloppy as hell, except for the parts Roy Seburn did, which were nice manic mandalas. Well, it was sloppy, but one thing you had to say for it; it was freaking lurid. The manifest, the destination sign in the front, read: "Furthur," with two *u*'s. . . ."

. . .

"[It was] as if somebody had given Hieronymous Bosch fifty buckets of Day-Glo paint and a 1939 International Harvester school bus and told him to go to it. On the floor by the bus is a 15-foot banner reading ACID TEST GRADUATION, and two or three of the Flag People are working on it. Bob Dylan's voice is raunching and rheuming and people are moving around, and babies are crying. I don't see them but they are somewhere in here, crying. Off to one side is a guy about 40 with a lot of muscles, as you can see because he has no shirt on—just a pair of khakis and some red leather boots on and his hell of a build—and he seems to be in a kinetic trance, flipping a small sledge hammer up in the air over and over, always managing to catch the handle on the way down with his arms and legs kicking out the whole time and his shoulders rolling and his head bobbing, all in a jerky beat as if somewhere Joe Cuba is playing 'Bang Bang'. . ."

. . .

"The sledge-hammer juggler rockets away—

"'Who is that?'

"'That's Cassady.'

"This strikes me as a marvelous fact. I remember Cassady. Cassady, Neal Cassady, was the hero, 'Dean Moriarty,' of Jack Kerouac's *On the Road*, the Denver Kid, a kid who was always racing back and forth across the U.S. by car, chasing, or outrunning, 'life,' and here is the same guy, now 40, in the garage, flipping a sledge hammer. . ."

. . .

"Kesey is young, serene, and his face is lineless, and round and smooth as a baby's as he sits for hours on end reading comic books, absorbed in the plunging purple Steve Ditko shadows of Dr. Strange attired in capes and chiaroscuro, saying: 'How could they have known that this gem was merely a device to bridge DIMENSIONS! It was a means to enter the dread PURPLE DIMENSION—from our own world! . . . Always seeing two Keseys. Kesey the Prankster and Kesey the organizer. Going through the steams of southern Alabama in late June and Kesey rises up from out of the comic books and becomes Captain Flag. He puts on a pink kilt, like a miniskirt, and pink socks and patent-leather shoes and pink sunglasses and wraps an American flag around his head like a big turban and holds it in place with an arrow through the back of it and gets up on top of the bus roaring through Alabama and starts playing the flute at people passing by. . . ."

PAINTING THE BUS IN PREPARATION FOR THE ACID TEST GRADUATION. (TED STRESHINSKY)

ACID TEST GRADUATION WITH (L. TO R.) KESEY, BABBS ON MICROPHONE, RON BEVIRT ON SECOND MICROPHONE. LAUREN KESSLER: "YES IT WAS ABOUT STAGING A GRAND GOOF, ABOUT BEING YOURSELF IN THE MOST OUTRAGEOUS WAY YOU'D CARE TO BE; YET IT WAS SOMETHING BIGGER.... WHAT WAS UNIQUE WAS THAT THEY WERE MAKING A CHOICE TO HAVE A GOOD TIME 'IN YOUR FACE.'... IN THE CONTEXT OF THE TIMES IT WAS AN UNUSUAL AND LIBERATING THING TO DO." (GENE ANTHONY)

ON THE BUS

KEN BABBS: "THE BEAUTY OF THE BUS WAS IT NEVER HAPPENED BEFORE AND NOBODY HAD ANY PRECONCEIVED IDEAS IN THEIR MINDS OF WHAT IT WAS ALL ABOUT. IF YOU DID SOMETHING LIKE THAT NOW, THEY'D JUST DISMISS YOU AS A BUNCH OF DRUGGED-OUT LOONIES BUT THEN THEY COULDN'T PIGEONHOLE US." (RON BEVIRT)

ORIGINS

Where did the "psychedelic revolution" begin? Certainly not with Ken Kesey and his Merry Band of Pranksters. Their role was to experiment in public and record it while it was happening, trailblazing a new frontier that attracted others. They didn't invent psychedelic drugs, they only used what was released from Pandora's box.

Science Discovers a Revolutionary New Headache Cure

To see where the psychedelic revolution really started, we have to go back to April 16, 1943, when LSD's creator, Albert Hofmann, mixed a batch of the stuff that he had synthesized from rye fungus five years earlier. He was hoping to find a cure for the common migraine and decided to do more research with a substance he called "LSD-25." While mixing it up, a small amount was absorbed through his fingertips. Notes in his diary record history's first acid trip:

> [What overcame me was] a remarkable but not unpleasant state of intoxication . . . characterized by an intense stimulation of the imagination, an altered state of awareness of the world. As I lay in a dazed condition with eyes closed there surged up from me a succession of fantastic, rapidly changing imagery of a striking reality and depth, alternating with a vivid, kaleidoscopic play of colors. This condition gradually passed off after about three hours.

Three days later Dr. Hofmann continued his solo experiment, taking 250 micrograms, and bicycling home through the streets of Zurich, Switzerland. That small dose had a large effect on the chemist:

> I had great difficulty in speaking coherently. My field of vision swayed before me, and objects appeared distorted like images in curved mirrors. I had the impression of being unable to move from the spot, although my assistant told me afterwards that we had cycled at a good pace. Occasionally I felt as if I were out of my body. . . . I thought I had died. My ego was suspended somewhere in space and I saw my body lying dead on the sofa. (*LSD: My Problem Child*, New York: McGraw-Hill, 1980)

By accident, Dr. Hofmann had discovered the kind of experience that mystics patiently search for for years, an encounter with altered, fresh perception. He didn't see it that way, however. When asked about LSD, Hofmann often referred to it as his "problem child."

Like many people with problem children, Hofmann was proud of his offspring. He saw many therapeutic applications for LSD and was happy to see it being used by scientists interested in how the mind works.

Still, LSD offered too many enticements to the spy community, mystics, and fun-seekers to keep it in the lab with common psychiatric drugs. Before long, the Central Intelligence Agency became interested in the possibilities of LSD as a mind control drug. Aroused by the scientific work of Dr. Werner Stoll (son of Sandoz president Arthur Stoll) the CIA began experiments of their own into uses of LSD.

They experimented on convicts, soldiers, the general populace, and even each other, in a research program known as ARTICHOKE. They tested many substances in this program, including morphine, mescaline, and even ether. But LSD was their favorite, perhaps because of the enormous effects that could come from so small a dose.

There was considerable experimentation being done outside the CIA, too. It seemed as though everyone was trying to figure out what to do with LSD.

One of these was Captain Alfred Hubbard, a wealthy, former World War II Army intelligence officer, whose enthusiastic sharing of the substance with members of his influential circle led him to be known as the "Johnny Appleseed of LSD". A unique character even for the surveillance community, he was a speculator in uranium mining, a one-time arms dealer, and a friend to industrialists and artists. He was what would eventually be called an "acid head," and he claimed to have seen his own conception while on acid, right down to his own parents having sex.

> It was the deepest mystical thing I've ever seen. I saw myself as a tiny mite in a big swamp with a spark of intelligence. I saw my mother and father having intercourse. It was all clear. (Martin A. Lee and Bruce Shlain, *Acid Dreams: The CIA, LSD and the Sixties Rebellion*, New York: Grove Press, 1985.)

In his search for people interested in this drug, he met and befriended Dr. Humphry Osmond, a psychiatrist at Weyburn Hospital in Saskatchewan, Canada, who was studying LSD's effect on the mentally ill. Dr. Osmond's writings would broaden the LSD community still further by reaching an influential author who would write a classic treatise on the psychedelic experience.

The "Miracle of Naked Existence"

Aldous Huxley's book-length essay, *The Doors of Perception*, was, for many, a literary door into the realm of psychedelics, that defined, perhaps as far as words can, the psychedelic experience. Huxley's own interest in psychedelics arose from reading a report on LSD written by Dr. Osmond. Fascinated, he offered himself as a guinea pig to the researcher, who in 1953, gave the author of *Brave New World* a healthy dose of LSD. The experience led the enthusiastic and articulate Huxley to expound on the marvels of the drug. In both *The Doors of Perception* and in public, the author discussed brain function, the ability of psychedelic drugs to open the mind's screening process to a virtual torrent of sensation, and the general "beatific" experience of it all. He didn't find that psychedelic drugs imitated psychosis, but instead that they opened the mind to a world of fresh perceptions.

> What Adam had seen on the morning of creation—the miracle, moment by moment, of naked existence . . . flowers shining with their own inner light and all but quivering under the pressure of the significance with which they were charged. . . . Words like 'grace' and 'transfiguration' came to mind. (*The Doors of Perception*, New York: Perennial Library, 1970)

Later, Huxley had an LSD experience with Captain Hubbard. It is said that Hubbard was so well-connected that the Vatican allowed him to administer LSD as part of the Catholic faith. Indeed, a newsletter item dated December 8, 1957, from Reverend J.E. Brown, a Catholic priest at the Cathedral of the Holy Rosary in Vancouver, seems to confirm that. From Reverend Brown's letter:

> We humbly ask Our Heavenly Mother the Virgin Mary, help of all who call upon Her to aid us to know and understand the true qualities of these psychedelics, the full capacities of man's noblest faculties and according to God's laws to use them for the benefit of mankind here and in eternity.

Years before Jerry Garcia began to lead Dead heads in celebration, the irrepressible Captain Al Hubbard served as the original "Captain Trips."

Tripping Draws Admirers: Life Magazine, Christopher Isherwood and Clare Boothe Luce . . .

By the mid-1950s, LSD was being used socially by intellectuals, scientists, and artists, such as Aldous Huxley, Dr. Humphry Osmond, philosopher Alan Watts and others in a Los Angeles social circle acquainted with Captain Hubbard. All became vigorous advocates of LSD's benefits. Huxley and Osmond were especially interested in challenging the prevailing belief that LSD induced insanity. While people who had repeatedly come close to insanity (alcoholics with delirium tremens, for instance) described that experience in awful terms, they usually spoke glowingly of their LSD experiences.

At this time, word of mouth began to draw others to sample the drug, for example, Henry Luce, the president of Time/Life, and his wife Clare Boothe Luce, had dropped acid with Huxley and the novelist Christopher Isherwood. LSD caused Luce to experience a vision of God while out on the golf course, and led him to "hear" heavenly music in a cactus garden while visiting the American West. Luce's *Life* Magazine soon showed editorial sympathies toward the psychedelic experience, publishing a seventeen-page article on "magic" mushrooms (written by R. Gordon Wasson, a vice-president of J.P. Morgan and Company) that is a virtual love song to the visions they induce:

We were never more awake, and the visions came whether our eyes were opened or closed. . . . They began with art motifs, angular such as might decorate carpets or textiles or wallpaper or the drawing board of an architect. They evolved into palaces with courts, arcades, gardens—resplendent palaces all laid over with semi-precious stones. . . . Later it was as though the walls of our house had dissolved, and my spirit had flown forth, and I was suspended in mid-air viewing landscapes of mountains, with camel caravans advancing slowly across the slopes, the mountains rising tier above tier to the very heavens. . . . The thought crossed my mind: could divine mushrooms be the secret that lay behind the ancient Mysteries? ("Seeking the Magic Mushroom," *Life*, May 27, 1957)

The article caused hundreds of people to head for Mexico in search of psychedelic bliss. Among those eventually lured to mushrooms by Wasson's article was Dr. Timothy Leary.

Dr. Leary Takes an Interest

Although head of clinical research and psychology at the Kaiser Foundation Hospital in Oakland, California, Leary was ready to devote his life to something entirely new. His first wife had committed suicide, he was divorced from his second one, and the thought of spending a lifetime in academia wasn't as appealing to him as it had once been.

On a trip to Mexico he took some magic mushrooms and had "the deepest religious experience of my life."

He returned to join Harvard University and establish a psilocybin research project. With him in this endeavor was Richard Alpert, an assistant professor of psychology. Alpert later became known as Baba Ram Dass, and is the India-mystic influenced American spiritual leader who is widely-known for his autobiographical book dealing with spirituality and enlightenment, "Be Here Now."

LSD as a Government Weapon

Through all of this, the CIA had a growing interest in LSD. Relatively small doses of the psychedelic could potentially affect the populations of whole cities, a capacity the CIA was interested in developing during the new era of cold war. They believed, for instance, that a dose properly introduced into a public water system might render a city helpless; that a smear of acid on a government official's drinking glass could make him act like a fool in public; that LSD given to a prisoner of war could erase his reluctance to talk.

There were many possible uses for LSD and other psychedelic drugs in the world of espionage. To explore these, the CIA financed the MK-ULTRA program in 1953, its purpose being to examine the mind-control possibilities of psychedelics.

MK-ULTRA experimenters tested LSD on each other as well as on unsuspecting fellow CIA employees. They dosed people during coffee breaks, Christmas parties, dinners, lunches, official retreats, at times administering these drugs when convenient, or simply interesting to do so.

Among the results: One CIA agent wept as he described his trip, saying he didn't want to leave the beautiful place that LSD took him to. An MK-ULTRA report said that the drug had made him "psychotic." Another fellow agent, it was reported, "Couldn't pull himself together." He said that his LSD trip was like a bad dream that wouldn't stop, one in which there was a monster out to get him in each car that passed.

These surreptitious experiments, practiced under the institutional respectability of government authority, backfired when a group of army technicians were dosed by CIA personnel at an informal work conference in the Maryland woods. A doctor slipped LSD into the dinner drinks of everyone present and then announced what he had done. It made for an evening of laughter and unintelligible talk and appeared to be a good time for everyone except Dr. Frank Olson, a biological warfare researcher.

There are certain people for whom LSD brings internal conflicts to the surface which might otherwise be surpressed, particularly if they are unprepared for the experience as Dr. Olson was. In the weeks following his unexpected LSD trip, he became unhappy, confused, and convinced that he was hearing voices and being harassed by the CIA. He became so despondent that he offered his resignation. In an attempt to undo some of the damage they had caused, CIA officials tried to get Dr. Olson counseling and they sent him to New York City accompanied by an agent. The CIA brought Olson to see Dr. Harold Abramson at Columbia University, who was one of their chief LSD researchers. He advised that Olson should receive psychiatric help, claiming that he was stuck in "a psychotic state. . . with delusions of persecution . . . crystallized by the LSD experience." Plans were made to send the dosed doctor to a sanitarium in Maryland.

But before that could happen, Olson died by hurtling through a closed, tenth-story Manhattan hotel window. His death was determined to be a suicide.

Without taking responsibility for his death, the CIA paid Olson's widow a full government pension. They were able to cover up the incident for twenty years, until it was uncovered by a Senate investigation of the agency's covert activities.

Still, CIA experimentation continued. A CIA operative set up a "safe house" in San Francisco and then paid prostitutes $100 a night to bring men to the apartment and dose them with LSD before having sex. The operative watched from behind a two-way mirror as dozens of men had sex with prostitutes under the influence of psychedelic drugs.

Military units were given LSD and asked to perform basic tasks like marching in formation, driving jeeps, and reading radar scopes. These experiments were filmed and shown later to demonstrate the incapacitating effects of LSD. By the mid-1960s, the U.S. Army alone had tested LSD on nearly 1500 soldiers.

You have to keep this all in mind before considering Ken Kesey and the Merry Pranksters. They didn't bring psychedelic drugs into the world. They merely helped make public what the CIA, the U.S. Army, Albert Hofmann, Aldous Huxley, Timothy Leary, and Clare Boothe Luce already knew: LSD re-opens doors of perception that modern life has closed.

Our Story Begins

For Ken Kesey those doors opened in 1959.

He came to Stanford University in 1958 after winning a Woodrow Wilson Fellowship, which was designed to help graduate students who had an interest in becoming college teachers. While at Stanford, Kesey opted to try out for the Stanford Writing Program using a football novel he was writing at the time as an entree into the department that novelist Wallace Stegner had built.

Kesey and his wife Faye found a house on Perry Lane, the bohemian section of Palo Alto. This was an entirely new environment for Kesey, a powerfully built 24-year-old country boy from Eugene, Oregon who had been a collegiate wrestler and drama student as an undergraduate at the University of Oregon.

Perry Lane was a literary world that was set apart even from Stanford University itself. Here Kesey found a suburban California bohemia, and friends such as Jane Burton, Ed

KEN KESEY: "I GET WEARY OF PEOPLE WHO USE PESSIMISM TO AVOID BEING RESPONSIBLE FOR ALL THE PROBLEMS OF OUR CULTURE. A MAN WHO SAYS 'WE'RE ON THE ROAD TO DISASTER' IS SELDOM TRYING TO WRENCH THE WHEEL AWAY FROM THE DRIVER. I PREFER THE TROUBLEMAKER." (RON BEVIRT)

McClanahan, Chloe Scott, Gurney Norman, and Ken Babbs, who would all later take part, to various degrees, in his Merry Prankster adventures. It was on Perry Lane that Kesey grew a beard and began playing folk songs on a guitar, here that Kesey ate his first marijuana brownie and got drunk for the second time (the first being his wedding day). It was also here that Kesey quit working on the football novel and started work on *Zoo*, a novel about a rodeo rider's son who moves to North Beach in San Francisco, where he experiences the communalism of the Beat generation. Ken Babbs was with him on many of his research trips to North Beach and recalls:

> One of the places we went to in North Beach was a coffee house called "The Place." Every Tuesday they had Free Speech Night. They had a balcony there and anyone who wanted to could get up and rant and rail about anything they wanted. I loved it. The same guys would always be in there, drinking coffee and beer and wine and listening

to the new speeches. They would sit there, never crack a smile or anything. They were the regulars, assessing new talent as it came in.

As part of the classroom experience, Kesey and the other Stanford writing students, who included Robert Stone and Larry McMurtry, read their works-in-progress to the rest of the class. But this year, 1959, Kesey was reading from *Zoo*, which didn't quite have the edge of his later work. Although it was largely responsible for getting him a graduate school scholarship, it remains unpublished, a student work that helped him develop the immense talent that was soon to reach fruition. A year later, after working in a mental hospital and taking part in drug experiments, Kesey would be reading unforgettable work that became *One Flew Over the Cuckoo's Nest*.

Drug Experiments Lead to the Writing of Cuckoo's Nest

Perry Lane and Stanford University were eye-openers for Kesey. In this academic setting he was exposed to literary disciplines that were new to him, just as he was exposed to people who broadened his world view. It was also here that Kesey elected to become one of the guinea pigs in what later proved to be part of the MK-ULTRA program. The CIA farmed out this top-secret program to a number of researchers, among them Dr. Leo Hollister at the Veterans Hospital in Menlo Park.

They were offering small cash stipends (under $100) for anyone who would partake of psychedelic drugs while researchers questioned, observed, and tested them. When Vic Lovell, a Perry Lane resident and psychology student, found out about the offer he convinced Kesey to enter the experimental program with him. Lovell had introduced Richard Alpert to marijuana and was himself curious about the effects of psychedelic drugs on the mind.

Over the next few weeks Kesey was given a variety of psycho-active drugs—from psilocybin and mescaline to LSD and the amphetamine IT-290. Some of it, he later told friends, was real bad, some real good, and some downright inspirational. But he believed that all would be better suited to use in a non-institutional setting.

In a short time, LSD found its way to Perry Lane, where Kesey and others were able to take this psychedelic drug in a more relaxed setting, where they could look at the world through these "doors of perception" without a hospital staff of white-coated researchers supervising the experience.

He discussed this fresh perspective drugs offered with the *Peninsula Times Tribune*, a Bay Area newspaper, in 1964:

> With these drugs, your perception is altered enough that you find yourself looking out of completely strange eyeholes. All of us have a great deal of our minds locked shut. And these drugs seem to be the key to open these locked doors.

In 1960, he took a summer job as a psychiatric aide at the Veterans Hospital. There he worked the graveyard shift, mopping floors, and talking to nurses and patients.

The Veterans Hospital afforded some of the best material for a novel that Kesey had ever seen. He was allowed to bring a typewriter to the nurses' station and write when his duties were completed. His experience in the hospital engaged his sympathies for the mentally ill, or people designated as such by the system and provided the theme of his first published work.

The characters in *One Flew Over the Cuckoo's Nest* were largely drawn from the patients and nurses surrounding him. But one night, after taking a dose of peyote, Kesey envisioned Chief Bromden, the schizophrenic Native American who narrates this incredible book about individuality and the system's desire to squash it flat.

Peyote helped Kesey discover the narrator (he admits to never having known such a character) just as it helped him clearly see the story line of man versus machine. As Kesey wrote in his Prankster anthology collection *Garage Sale:*

> [It] was after choking down eight of the little cactus plants that I wrote the first three pages. These pages remained almost completely unchanged through the numerous rewrites the book went through, and from this first spring I drew all the passion and perception the narrator spoke with during the ten months writing that followed.

The next ten months were extraordinary ones for Kesey. He worked hard at *Cuckoo's Nest*, often writing at night when he could be totally alone and then reading his work in class at Stanford. For much of the semester Kesey's writing professor was Malcolm Cowley, who had discovered Jack Kerouac and who had edited the works of William Faulkner and Ernest Hemingway. Cowley insisted on a supportive atmosphere in class, reminding his students not to become too cut-throat with their peers lest they have their throats cut in retribution. He also

KEN KESEY'S SON, JED, AND WIFE, FAYE, LOOK THROUGH ONE OF THE WINDOWS OF THE BUS. (RON BEVIRT)

KEN KESEY'S DAUGHTER SHANNON (LEFT) AND SON ZANE. (RON BEVIRT)

is responsible for this maxim, intended to help maintain a constructive atmosphere of respect, among students: "Remember, it is just as hard to write a bad novel as it is a good one."

This was the best environment that a young novelist like Kesey could hope for. Bearing testimony to this was the subsequent success of his classmates in the program, who included novelists Larry McMurtry, Ed McClanahan, Gurney Norman, Peter Beagle, Ken Babbs and Robert Stone. With supportive friends, an intellectual community, good material to draw from, and LSD to help him see it more clearly, his talent soon began to flourish.

KEN BABBS. (RON BEVIRT)

ORIGINS—ORAL HISTORIES...

... In which various Merry Pranksters and fellow travellers describe the idyllic technicolor paradise of bohemian community that formed around Oregonian athlete Ken Kesey and his friends from the now-legendary Stanford University Creative Writing Program at the end of the Eisenhower Era. . . .

Kesey begins his participation in psychedelic drug experiments at the Veterans Hospital in Menlo Park, California and takes a job there as a psychiatric aide, where he receives his inspiration to write a novel, eventually titled *One Flew Over the Cuckoo's Nest*, which lifts him to the heights of literary celebrity. . . .

Always at the center of a scene of literary discussion, carousing, and exploration of mind-altering substances, Kesey finds that notoriety and riches enable these activities to take place on a larger scale. He writes a second novel, *Sometimes a Great Notion*, and begins to look beyond writing to invent ways to "live life as a novel."

This section features commentary from:
GURNEY NORMAN—Stanford classmate of Kesey's, currently a novelist, author of *Divine Right's Trip*.
MALCOLM COWLEY—former Stanford creative writing instructor, legendary Viking Press editor (speaking in a 1977 *Northwest Quarterly* interview).
ROBERT STONE—Stanford classmate, currently a novelist, author of *Dog Soldiers* and *Children of Light*.
KEN BABBS—a.k.a. "The Intrepid Traveller."
RON BEVIRT—a.k.a. "Hassler," Prankster photographer.
KEN KESEY—a.k.a. "The Chief" (speaking with Gordon Lish in a 1963 interview in *Genesis West* magazine).
ED MCCLANAHAN—Stanford classmate, currently a novelist and teacher, author of *Famous People I Have Known*.
GORDON LISH—Stanford friend of Kesey's, currently a fiction writer, teacher, and editor at Alfred A. Knopf, Inc., publishers.

GURNEY NORMAN: It in every way was the absolute equivalent to any literary scene that ever existed anywhere. I don't concede anything. I'm in no way envious of Paris in the twenties because we had Palo Alto in the sixties.

I was sitting in a room twice a week with Malcolm Cowley and going to his house for drinks and listening to his personal reminiscences of Hemingway and Dos Passos. Herbert Gold, who was in his first rush of true fame in 1960, was teaching. Frank O'Connor was one of our teachers. And then, of course, there was Wallace Stegner, who wasn't teaching that year but we still went up to his house for these very elegant but authentic home-feeling occasions that would be in his living room.

For instance, we went over there one time to meet Robert Frost. He was almost ninety at the time and was resting in the back room. We were convened, and when it came time for him to make his appearance we all stood up—probably fifteen people—in kind of an improvised reception line, and Mr. Stegner introduced him to each of us.

He came over to me and Mr. Stegner said, "Mr. Norman," and Frost held out his hand. What a moment!

Three months after that I'm watching the inauguration of John Kennedy on TV and there was Robert Frost next to the new president! It was like suddenly feeling that your life had been elevated or expanded to a mythic dimension. The man I shook hands with three months before was now part of Kennedy's inauguration!

MALCOLM COWLEY: It was a pretty brilliant class that year, including as it did some professional writers already launched on their careers. Larry McMurtry, for instance, was working on what I think was his second novel, *Leaving Cheyenne*. He was a light, sallow, bespectacled cowboy who wore Texas boots and spoke in a pinched variety of the West Texas drawl. Gradually, I learned that he had read almost everything in English literature, besides a great deal in French, and that he had written a dissertation on the scabrous poetry of John Wilmot, Earl of Rochester. Larry supplemented his Stanford fellowship by finding rare books on the ten cent tables of Salvation Army outlets and reselling them to dealers; *Book Prices Current* was his bible.

ROBERT STONE: I got out of the Navy in 1958 and sort of drifted around for awhile. I got my high school equivalency in the Navy and I applied to New York University, but I was working at the New York Daily News at night and I had to drop out because the workload was too heavy.

I got married and we moved to New Orleans. I did all sorts of stuff down there. I got a union card with the Merchant Marine and I shipped out a couple of times. I did a little bit of everything. I helped take the 1960 census and even did telephone sales.

Then we moved back to New York where we were taking turns baby-sitting and working. One day I was walking down the street and I ran into a professor of mine from NYU, a poet named Mack Rosenthal. He told me about the Wallace Stegner Writing Fellowship at Stanford. I was writing this novel at the time that was set in New Orleans and I decided to, what the hell, go for the beans. I sent in the first chapters of the novel to Stegner and a few months later I found out that I got the fellowship.

MALCOLM COWLEY: Peter S. Beagle was only 21, with plump cheeks and a solemn boyish smile, but The Viking Press had already published his successful first novel, *A Fine and Private Place*. I took a special interest in Peter, since I was a literary adviser for Viking and since I knew and liked his two famous uncles, the painters Raphael and Moses Soyer. There were other gifted students in the class. I remember James Baker Hall, Judith Rascoe, Arvin Brown, Gurney Norman, and Joanna Ostrow, who was the most beautiful woman I encountered in twenty years of teaching.

ROBERT STONE: It was an amazing thing for us because we came from the Lower East Side of New York—got on a train and went out to Palo Alto, California. It was like going from black and white to technicolor. Northern California in 1962 was a bloody paradise. It was the most easy-going, pleasant, civilized, laid-back place you can imagine. To get out there, to be there, to settle into those surroundings was really the best of times.

GURNEY NORMAN: The fall of 1960 was a very special season. It was a political year. It was the New Frontier; it was Kennedy. The political scene was cooking in a radical way in the Bay Area because the House Committee on Un-American Activities was holding hearings, and they were summoning college professors before them and denouncing them, ruining their lives and reputations. There were demonstrations against the hearings. It was a highly charged moment in American history.

NOVELIST GURNEY NORMAN, A STANFORD CLASSMATE OF KESEY AND AUTHOR OF *DIVINE RIGHT'S TRIP.* (RON BEVIRT)

It was a highly charged period in the writing class, too.

ROBERT STONE: I turned up for class that first day and I found myself sitting across the table from this guy wearing blue suede shoes and a two-toned country-and-western jacket and wrap-around shades and a pompadour and I thought, "Christ, what kind of yo-yo is this?" Being a New York boy, and thinking I was sharp, I couldn't figure out what this hick was doing there.

The guy turned out to be Ed McClanahan. It was Ed who first brought me around to Perry Lane, and it was through Ed that I met Kesey and the people who were on the Lane at the time.

A lot of them were people who were going to be on the bus a couple of years later. Jane Burton was there and Vic Lovell, to whom *Cuckoo's Nest* is dedicated, lived there and of course Gurney was around on weekends. Babbs was still in Vietnam but he would show up later.

KEN BABBS: Kesey had graduated from the U. of O. in 1958, but he had worked in Hollywood for a year, trying to get into the film industry. Then he applied for a Woodrow Wilson Fellowship and got it, so he and I were both there that first year. And then the next year he got one of the Wallace Stegner Fellowships. I was in ROTC, so I had to go into the Marine Corps. That first year he was writing a book called *Zoo* about the North Beach Beat scene. It had its moments, but I don't remember it much. *Cuckoo's Nest* didn't happen until I had gone into the Marines.

MALCOLM COWLEY: The class of fifteen assembled in the Jones Room at a huge oval table. One student would read his work aloud and others would offer comments. My problem at the head of the table was how to get the class working together. I believed that young writers learn more from one another than they do from an older instructor. I knew that their comments on stories revealed two contradictory impulses: first, to assert their egos by putting down their rivals; second, to advance the cause of good writing in an unselfish fashion by making useful suggestions. Aggression and *agape*. My tactic was always to put down the putter-downers and always to encourage the suggestions. In a good class like the one at Stanford in 1960, *agape* won out, jealousies were submerged, and stories were sometimes vastly improved in their second and third drafts.

GURNEY NORMAN: Central to the class experience was the fact that Kesey was bringing in chapters of *Cuckoo's Nest*. Every three weeks

WRITER ROBERT STONE ON THE CAMPUS AT STANFORD: "SOMETIMES I FEEL LIKE I WENT TO A PARTY IN 1963 AND IT SORT OF SPILLED OUT THE DOOR AND INTO THE STREET AND COVERED THE WORLD." (RON BEVIRT)

or so, Ken would bring in a new chapter. He was in the throes of working at the hospital while he cranked out these chapters that had a very odd perspective and point-of-view that came from inside the mind of this Indian narrator.

There was a lot of talk at this time about drugs like mushrooms and peyote, so we began to think about Kesey's work as a psychedelic novel.

To make extra money, Kesey signed up for drug experiments at the Veterans Hospital in Menlo Park. Kesey and other volunteers sat in white rooms in the hospital's psychiatric ward, taking LSD, Ditran, mescaline, and IT-290. While on psychedelics he could ponder the nature of insanity, which helped him as he struggled to write *Cuckoo's Nest*. "While on the drugs I could see where these guys were coming from, and I could see that they weren't so crazy," he said. What was crazy, Kesey believed, was taking these drugs in a sterile environment while the white coats periodically drew blood and checked blood pressure. As he told the *Peninsula Times Tribune* in 1987: "We were asked by the government, 'Hey, go into that little box over there. There's something in that little box that we don't have the hair to go into.' So they hired a bunch of college students to go in there . . . then they said, 'Don't let them back in that box!'" Kesey decided to liberate some of the drugs for home experimentation.

NOVELIST ED MCCLANAHAN: "I DECIDED NOT TO GO [ON THE BUS TRIP]. WE HAD TWO KIDS AND I THOUGHT THAT THERE WAS THE LIKELIHOOD THAT EVERYBODY WAS GOING TO COME BACK IN IRONS. I NOW THINK SOMEBODY WAS WATCHING OVER THEM, I'LL TELL YOU THAT." (RON BEVIRT)

RON BEVIRT: Somebody at the Veterans Hospital there had gotten some kind of government grant and they were studying the effects of psychedelics on volunteers.

And Vic Lovell, who was a member of the scene there who was a graduate student in psychology, had plugged into this scene somehow and knew about it. He said to Ken, "You should really go out and do this, you know. Taking these drugs is far out."

ROBERT STONE: Kesey had been a volunteer in these psychedelic experiments when he was working as an orderly at the Veterans Administration Hospital, so he just brought a lot of it back to Perry Lane. We saw it partly as fun and partly as spiritual adventure. But the government saw it differently. The story was that they were experimenting with it in terms of therapeutic use, but there seemed to be a military connection, too. I think they wanted to use it as some kind of weapon, something you could put into an enemy country's water supply.

RON BEVIRT: Basically, their way of doing this was they put you in a white tiled room and they would come in and take samples of your blood. Then they would give you the drug. One or two hours went by and they kept coming in and taking blood.

So here's Ken in this psychedelicized state but the scene sucks. So he notes where they put the bottle in the drawer and when they go out of the room, he goes over and dumped some in his pocket for his own use later on. Simultaneously, Timothy Leary and Richard Alpert were doing their own thing at Harvard. Since Alpert had been an instructor at Stanford, we connected through him.

KEN KESEY: Another world happened. I took mescaline, psilocybin, IT-290, LSD, and some bad-scene stuff that produces a condition intended to demonstrate to the whining neurotic how much worse off he can be. I'm grateful for this experience. It showed me scenes I'd otherwise never know. I had a tape recorder with me, free access to most of the place, and plenty of time to lie on my back watching whatever was moving around on the ceiling or [looking at] the other guys who were watching their own scenes. It slowly became evident that there was some awful and unique logic going on, just as real, in some ways, as your other world. It's very difficult to explain.

R O N B E V I R T : LSD is really a catalyst for psychic perception, a way of getting to a whole lot of profound stuff. Taking psychedelics is not just a lark.

M A L C O L M C O W L E Y : His first drafts must have been written at top speed; they were full of typing errors, as if the words had come piling out of a Greyhound bus too fast to have their clothes brushed. Later, Kesey would redo the manuscript and correct most of the misspellings. He had his visions, but he didn't have the fatal notion of some Beat writers that the first hasty account of a vision was a sacred text not to be tampered with. He revised, he made deletions and additions; he was working with readers in mind. I continued to be excited by Kesey's work as the manuscript grew longer (though I couldn't share his faith in the Randle P. McMurphy system of psychotherapy). I remember sending enthusiastic reports to Viking. A year later I was delighted when the manuscript arrived in the Viking office, this time with a title: *One Flew Over the Cuckoo's Nest.*

G U R N E Y N O R M A N : It was also a very political novel. I mean, here's a writer who is looking at American society as a loony bin. And the hero is someone who is messing with the system, and the narrator—the consciousness and the soul of the book—is a Native American whose final act is to rip out the controls of the system and use it to smash a hole in the wall of the hospital, which creates an image of a force that smashes through the barriers of American thinking. The novel has to be read that way.

Anyway, so here we are sitting in this class reading this stuff in manuscript at the beginning of a decade where literally a hole was blown through the walls of the Eisenhower mindset. The fifties had been a suffocating time and suddenly everything was being blown apart. As Kesey was reading those chapters, we knew that there was something pretty special about them.

M A L C O L M C O W L E Y : I don't remember any comments that Kesey made. I do remember that he looked stolid and self-assured as he sat near the other end of the table. He had the build of a plunging halfback, with big shoulders and a neck like the stump of a Douglas fir. Chapters of his novel were read aloud in class and they aroused a mixed but generally admiring response. The instructor was excited by having found something original. Later Kesey showed me the whole of the unfinished manuscript and we discussed it in private sessions. Did I contribute anything? "Not even a sentence" is the answer; the book is Kesey's from first word to the last. Probably I pointed out passages that didn't "work," that failed to produce a desired effect on the reader. Certainly I asked questions, and some of these may have helped to clarify Kesey's notions of how to go about solving his narrative problems, but the solutions were always his own.

KEN KESEY: I've found psychedelics to be keys to worlds that have always existed, that have to be talked about. The kaleidoscopic pictures, the geometrics of humanity, that one experiences under, say, mescaline, aren't concealed in the white crystals inside the gelatin capsule. They are always in the mind. In the world. Already. The chemical allows the picture to be seen. To know the world you need to see as many sides of it as possible. And this sometimes means using microscopes, telescopes, spectroscopes, even kaleidoscopes. . . . Drugs didn't create those descriptions any more than Joyce's eyeglasses created *Ulysses*. They merely help one to see the paper more clearly.

MALCOLM COWLEY: From the beginning he had his narrator in the person of Chief Bromden, a schizophrenic Indian who pretends to be deaf and dumb. [Kesey] had his own crazy visions—induced by eating peyote, as he later explained—and these could be ascribed to Chief Bromden. Thus, when the Indian looks at Big Nurse, "She's swelling up, swells till her back's splitting out of the white uniform and she's let her arms section out long enough to wrap around the three of them five, six times . . . she blows up bigger and bigger, big as a tractor. So big I can smell the machinery inside the way you smell a motor pulling too big a load." That hallucinated but everyday style, smelling of motor oil, was something new in fiction. Kesey's narrative problem, the central one, was how to use Chief Bromden's visions as the medium for telling an essentially simple, dramatic, soundly constructed story.

ED MCCLANAHAN: In the fall of 1961 I finished writing the piece that I was submitting for the fellowship, which, by the way, was a novella that 21 years later was published as my first novel, *The Natural Man*. Anyway, I finished writing that because I really wanted to apply for a Stegner Fellowship. Plus, I just couldn't wait to get out of Oregon State where I was teaching all of these freshman composition classes.

A poet named John Hazlett was teaching at Oregon State at the time, and he decided one afternoon that we should go over to Eugene and meet Ken. I had read a review of *Cuckoo's Nest* and decided that I would like to meet him.

Kesey was up there that summer working as a logger to get material for *Sometimes a Great Notion*, which he was working on at the time. We met him at "The Sparr," which was a loggers' bar. We spent a couple of hours with him, drinking beer, and then I drove him home in my MG and met Faye.

I told him I had just applied for a Stegner Fellowship and was quite sure I was going to get it, and that I would see him down in California when he got back. I did get the fellowship, so I went down to look for a house and rented a place on Alpine Road, within walking distance of Perry Lane.

GURNEY NORMAN: Perry Lane was basically old housing left over from World War I. When the United States got into the war, the Stanford farm was taken over as an Army camp to train soldiers. They put up this shotgun housing. They just lay these little framed cabins in a row and a squad of soldiers would live there. Those shacks, the ones that survived, became the Perry Lane community.

A bohemian village grew up there. From 1920 until they were torn down, the houses were occupied by artists, writers, and people trying to live cheaply. Over the years they had been modernized, fixed, and built-up. By the late sixties you had Stanford literary types living there, drinking wine and having intellectual discussions. It was into the middle of this community that psychedelic drugs were introduced.

ROBERT STONE: It was a real tribal scene at Perry Lane. It was tribal in part because we were amusing ourselves with these experimental drugs. The situation is hard to imagine because nobody really knew much about the stuff. I think a number of us had read Huxley's books, and also some of the artists in the twenties in Europe, like Joan Miró, had used psychedelics, so there was an artistic and bohemian tradition for the use of psychedelics.

Still, we were rather pleased with ourselves. We were young and thought that we were just incredibly sophisticated and bohemian to be doing all this far-out stuff.

Plus, you have to remember that nobody was playing cops and robbers with us at this point over the use of psychedelics. It was extremely pleasant. This was our world and we kept our world small and got very close.

GURNEY NORMAN: Ken is so gregarious that it was totally natural for his home on Perry Lane to become an after-hours hangout for the people in the seminar. Frequently, the seminar would go on half the afternoon. We would then go to the campus coffee shop for two more hours of talking and then the real hardcore element—one of whom I became as time went on—would go back to Ken's house where Faye would cook up rice and beans, and it would go on into the night and turn into wine-drinking and guitar-playing. That's how we gravitated to Ken's house, and his house became the center of one side of the socializing among campus writers.

MALCOLM COWLEY: After turning over the advanced writing course to Frank O'Connor—in private life Michael O'Donovan—I had spent the winter quarter at Stanford with less challenging assignments. Michael was a dear man with an Irish temper who wouldn't stand for nonsense. He couldn't have felt much sympathy for Kesey's narrator or his style or his hero. I heard that Kesey had stopped attending classes in the Jones Room and was persuading others to stay away too, sometimes by inviting them to his house on Perry Lane and keeping them there with drinks and conversation until the class was over. He had become the man whom other young rebels tried to imitate, almost like Hemingway in Montparnasse during the 1920s.

ED MCCLANAHAN: We used to get together and have these writers' sessions. Originally it was Kesey and I and Vic Lovell and whoever happened to be around. The others didn't have to be writers, but they wanted to hear us read our stuff. Then I brought Bob Stone, because he and I were in Stegner's class together. Bob and I hit it off real quick and became friends right away. It was very funny, because Ken didn't trust Bob Stone. He thought Bob was a Communist. Ken told me one time that he didn't want Bob to come to these meetings anymore. I said, "Oh yes you do, you just wait, you'll like him." Bob kept coming and the two became really tight.

GURNEY NORMAN: These parties were full of life and laughter. It is hard to see anything in the least bit decadent about them. They were very sweet and dear and above all, extremely literary.

Drugs were a spice in the cake for Kesey. He'd rather talk about Melville and Moby Dick than about drugs.

ED MCCLANAHAN: Larry McMurtry was out of the program then but he was living in San Francisco, so he started coming to these sessions, too.

They were great scenes. Everybody sitting on the floor. Usually there would be wine and beer. The weed hadn't come out yet, not to say there wasn't plenty of smoking going on, but we didn't do it openly, that was maybe six months off. People would slip off to the bathroom sometimes, but dope hadn't come out of the closet yet, or out of the bathroom would be a more appropriate way of putting it.

ROBERT STONE: The first time I did any psychedelics was when I was still living in New York. There was an espresso house on East Sixth Street that sold peyote buttons and was run by a guy named Barron, who was a follower of Ayn Rand. His espresso shop had no name but it had a dollar sign hanging out in front of the window.

This guy sold peyote, which was legal then. He ordered it from a place in Texas called "Smith's Cactus Ranch." We did everything we could to hold that bitter stuff down in our stomachs, but we never succeeded in getting terribly high.

I got much higher the first time I did peyote with the Perry Lane

JANE BURTON—STANFORD
GRADUATE STUDENT, PERRY LANE
RESIDENT, AND FUTURE
PRANKSTER. (RON BEVIRT)

crowd. They got a bunch of peyote and dried it out in somebody's stove. Then they got pharmaceutical gelatin capsules and stuck the stuff into the capsules.

I thought I knew about this stuff from my New York experiences so I took twelve capsules, which turned out to be kind of a mistake.

We went to San Francisco to hear John Coltrane and as soon as I was sitting there listening to Coltrane, I was seeing the music. I think the word for it is synesthesia. I was seeing Coltrane's music. I could see breath in these big jagged waves of frost; I could see the percussion. It was just too much for me so I had to leave the club.

We split up in Chinatown. The rest of the crowd went from Coltrane to Lenny Bruce, but my wife and I wandered around the streets. I was undone. I don't know what it looked like from the outside, but from the inside it was pretty crazy.

Perry Lane was always a teeming party scene, but the introduction of psychedelics changed the nature of activity on the Lane. LSD joined forces with venison to make a psychedelic stew that made those who ate it high and full. The peyote buttons ordered from Smith's Cactus Ranch were

eaten freely on Perry Lane. These drugs were legal then, so those curious about the psychedelic dimension were free to roam.

MALCOLM COWLEY: I paid perhaps two visits to Perry Lane, which was the Left Bank of Stanford, but the visit I remember was on the night when Kesey and his wife were throwing a big party. Most of the advanced writing class was there, with other friends of the Keseys, including Vic Lovell, a graduate student with bold notions about psychology and a ducktail haircut. On a table by the window was a huge bowl of green punch from which clouds of mist kept rising. Kesey explained that the punch was brewed with Kool-Aid and dry ice; the mist was carbon dioxide. "It looks like the sort of punch that Satan would serve," I said while politely accepting half a cupful. Was it the famous punch that Kesey had spiked with LSD? I haven't the faintest notion because I never drained my cup. Instead, I wandered out to the kitchen, where my wife was talking with Faye Kesey and admiring the baby. I fell into conversation with Ken's grandmother. "If you don't like punch," she said, "I brought along a bottle of bootleg whiskey from Arkansas." "That suits me just fine," I said, taking a pull at the bottle. By that time the crowd around the punch bowl was growing noisy. Arvin Brown, who drank several cupfuls of the green stuff, tells me that he didn't recover full consciousness for 24 hours.

ROBERT STONE: We were often stoned at these parties, so just little bits and pieces here and there come back because we were all out of our minds. I do remember one game we played at the "Demise Party" [which was held just before Perry Lane residents were evicted so the houses could be demolished]. Gurney organized a bunch of us into a giant cat's cradle. We were all stoned on acid and trying to keep track of where everyone was at the same time. I remember Gurney yelling, "All the thumbs raise their hands."

Most of the reviews for *One Flew Over the Cuckoo's Nest*, upon publication in 1962, were an author's dream. The *New York Times* described it as "a glittering parable of good and evil." *Saturday Review* said, "His storytelling is so effective, his style so impetuous, his grasp of the characters so certain that the reader is swept along in McMurphy's boisterous wake . . . he has written a large, robust book." While *The New Yorker's* criticism of the book's style as "paste-pot colloquial" sounded a discordant note, the

New York *Herald Tribune* was more representative: "Undoubtedly there will be controversy over some of the material in Ken Kesey's novel, but there can be none about his talent. His is a powerful book about a mental institution, written with sustained vitality and force which hold the reader until the final word." Almost overnight, Kesey became a literary star, and a media celebrity.

GURNEY NORMAN: In 1961 I went into the Army. I remember distinctly being in the Army and opening *Time* magazine and there's a picture of Kesey leaning against a tree on Perry Lane. In other words, a year after hearing his manuscript in class, out it comes.

Suddenly Kesey is overnight-famous. There are incredible reviews from everywhere. It was just a blockbuster, so it wasn't just fame, but mega-fame coming down. At the same time, there was something in the book that shot out and caused it to become a popular success among people who didn't even read these reviews.

Kesey's ascendancy brought changes to life on Perry Lane. But although he had become a celebrity, certain aspects remained the same.

GURNEY NORMAN: I took my Army training and where did they send me? Fort Ord in Monterey. So I was out of Stanford in June and by February of the next year I was right back in Palo Alto.

I was a lieutenant in charge of giving basic training to infantry soldiers. I was there all week running around doing my little duties at Fort Ord, and then Saturday at noon I would take off my Army clothes, put on my civilian clothes, and drive straight for Perry Lane and get on with being a bohemian. Along with Babbs I was one of the very first soldiers who was a weekend bohemian.

In the meantime, Ken had hit this big lick with *Cuckoo's Nest*. So it was my fate to be in the Army and his to suddenly be a damn star. People like Neal Cassady were looking Ken up and Kirk Douglas was coming around. But somehow, to Ken's credit, he kept writing. I don't know how he did this. On one of my first visits back to Perry Lane in February, Ken was throwing a party. There was drunken dancing going on, but Ken said, "Gurney, come out to the back shack, I want to show you something." We went out there and he handed me the first fifty pages of *Sometimes a Great*

Notion. "See what you think of this." So there in the middle of this party, Ken wanted to talk about fiction.

ED MCCLANAHAN: One very memorable thing that happened to me had nothing to do with the writing groups. Ken came over and brought me a big wad of manuscript one day that was just as rough as a cob—a lot of handwriting on it and full of misspellings and weird typos. It was a lot of material—about fifty pages—and he said, "Read this and tell me what you think about it."

Over the next day or so I read it [*Sometimes a Great Notion*], and it was really a powerhouse bunch of stuff. I went to take it back to him and he said, "Well, what do you think?" I said, "God, it's really terrific, but there is one thing I don't understand. In that first scene there, what is that arm hanging out over the river?" He said, "Shit, I don't know whose arm it is, that's what I'm writing this book for, to find out." I think it's true, he really didn't know what he was writing until he wrote.

ROBERT STONE: I remember the first time I met Hassler [Ron Bevirt]. We were all down at the place that became Esalen, down at Big Sur, and we were in the hot tub—my wife, my sister-in-law, the McClanahans, and a whole bunch of us from Perry Lane—and I remember Gurney showing up with Hassler, who was then his fellow officer. I remember Hassler finding out that what was going to happen was that he was going to get into this big tub of sulfur water with a bunch of people—men, women and children—who were naked. He had just never done anything like that before. I remember how embarrassed and sort of perplexed he was at the licentiousness of getting into this hot tub and looking at the ocean and smoking marijuana.

RON BEVIRT: I went to Washington University in St. Louis, and I was a literature major there, and I was interested in writing. I had read a review in *Time* magazine of *Cuckoo's Nest* that had a picture of Kesey. Somehow, when I saw that review of *Cuckoo's Nest*, there was some kind of psychic thing there. I don't mean to make too much of it, but *On the Road* had made a big impression on me. It was such a clarion call for a generation, a bursting of the bonds of the time that had constrained us.

Somehow, *On the Road* was like a scent of some exquisite perfume of the soul. Later on at Perry Lane, when Cassady showed up, everything hooked up. It was like it was meant to be. My feeling was that I had found my people.

With the notoriety came a new group of characters, among them Neal Cassady. Called the "holy primitive" by poet Allen Ginsberg, Cassady was the model for Dean Moriarty, the free-wheeling, talk-a-lot, drive-a-lot, beat philosopher in Jack Kerouac's *On the Road*. Fresh from a two-year jail stint at San Quentin, where he did time for possession of a single joint of marijuana, Cassady was drawn to the Prankster scene the way a divining rod is drawn to water.

NEAL CASSADY. ROBERT STONE RECALLS: "NEAL WAS A LOT LIKE THAT CHARACTER BRANDO DID IN *THE WILD ONE*, THE REAL FORTIES HIPSTER . . . HE WAS A GUY WHO HAD OBVIOUSLY SEEN THE UNDERSIDE OF AMERICA."
(RON BEVIRT)

ED MCCLANAHAN: The first time I remember Neal Cassady showing up was when we were having one of these reading groups over at my house on Alpine Road. We had a fairly roomy living room. This was in January of 1963 and Larry McMurtry was reading that day with several people from the class at Stanford.

The room was full of folks listening to the stories, probably one of the biggest groups we've ever had. It seems to me that Larry was reading a piece from *Leaving Cheyenne* when suddenly there was this big roar of an old banger of an automobile out front, car doors slamming and what-have-you. The doors burst open into the room and in comes Cassady.

In the "Popeye the Sailor" comic strip they would every once in a while show a huge crowd, and all you would see was all these little knobby bald heads, and if Popeye wanted to go up front he would just walk over the tops of the bald heads. That's what Neal did. He didn't stomp on anybody's head, but he sort of danced over them and just came to the front of the room.

As I recall he didn't have a shirt on and he was just dancing and moving and talking incessantly. . . .

I have a description of that first meeting in my book, *Famous People I Have Known*. There's about a page of what I kind of recall as being Neal's rap at the time. It read more or less like this:

Just passing through folks, don't mind us, my schedule just happened to coincide with Mr. Kesey's here and all that redundancy, you understand, not to mention the works of Alfred Lord Tennyson and the worst of the Thorns of Shiller, hunting and pecking away there as they did, of course, in so far as where you draw the line, that is but in any case, I believe it was at, let me see, Sebring, yes, when Fontgiere with the exhaust valves wide open and the pet cops, too, that you've sometime seen starting with Wadsworth, you see, and working backwards in the traditional fashion straight through "Plan of the Elder" and "Beyond," though it's much the same with fusion of the existential and the transcendental, or if you will, the universal and the transmission as in the case of the 1940 flat-head Cadillac Eight, why you just naturally get your velocity mixed up with your veracity, of course.

And who knows what that's cost us, so I'll just say 'how do you do' to my friend Mr. Kesey and then we'll be on our way. Have to get there in plenty of time, you understand.

From then on Neal started turning up pretty often, and I got to know him. I don't claim to have been on the intimate, but I got to know Neal pretty well and really liked him.

GORDON LISH: The night I graduated from University of Arizona I packed up my wife and kids, and we got into a little Ford Fairlane convertible with a top that didn't go up, fifty dollars in our pockets, and a four wheel U-Haul, and went driving through the desert to North Beach to see Dean Moriarty.

I had never been to California, but I thought there was a beach at North Beach and a Dean Moriarty! I mean, I was an insane person. I'm someone who thought that the characters in the Caulfield family in *Catcher in the Rye* were real people running around. I thought if I could dump myself in the right place I could meet them.

I read three books in my life that really took me by the neck— Salinger's *Catcher in the Rye* and *Nine Stories*, and Kerouac's *On the Road*. I just swallowed them hook, line, and sinker, and went looking for Dean Moriarty.

When we arrived at North Beach I discovered that this was no beach but rather an avenue with side streets. I had a 24-hour party. I walked around to places like the Anxious Asp and the Co-Existence Bagel Shop with one of my kids on my shoulders asking if anybody had seen Dean Moriarty. People would look at me like I was a lunatic.

I didn't actually meet "Dean Moriarty," or Neal Cassady, until a couple of years later when I met Ken Kesey. I met Kesey because I was starting a literary magazine called *Genesis West*. I was a fan of a guy named Allen Temko, who wrote stories for some literary magazines that I read. I stared scouring the Bay Area phone books to find this guy and I couldn't find any Temko save a "Phillip Temko" that lived in San Jose. I called him and he said, "Oh, that's my cousin you're looking for. His number is unlisted and he's not writing fiction anymore. Why do you want him?"

I explained that I was starting a literary magazine and he said that he used to teach English at the University of Oregon and was having a party with a lot of writers.

We get down there and I start trading life stories with this Temko. I tell him that I did some wrestling when I was in high school and had been in the nut house twice. He tells me that he used to coach wrestling at the University of Oregon and one of his star wrestlers was at Stanford where he was writing a book about a nut house. Maybe we should get together, he suggests.

ROBERT STONE: In the period of three or four years of working very hard, [Kesey] turned out two very important novels. And then he was ready to quit writing for a while. He noticed something that I didn't, that a revolution was in progress. Ken saw the revolution coming and felt that he had a social mission. He was going to use the power of his personality to do something special.

I didn't realize that this would take such a non-literary form. I knew that he had enormous presence and personality. He really liked coping

WRITER AND EDITOR GORDON LISH IN A 1962 PHOTO. LISH FIRST MET KESEY AT STANFORD: "KESEY WAS A WRITER OF IMPECCABLE DISCIPLINE WHEN I FIRST KNEW HIM, A TRUE CHAMPION, A TRUE WINNER, A MOST ADMIRABLE LITERARY ARTIST, WHOSE RELATIONS WITH THE PAGE WERE OF THE HIGHEST ORDER.... [BUT] I THINK HIS HEART WAS TAKEN OUT OF HIM WHEN THE NEW YORK ESTABLISHMENT DID NOT FALL ALL OVER THEMSELVES ON [*SOMETIMES A GREAT NOTION*]..." (BARBARA LISH)

and leading and acting and had great gifts for all of these things. Before long, it was easy to see that he was moving in a direction that was not purely literary.

KEN KESEY: Unless you get up very near that precipice where you're likely to make a fool of yourself, you're not showing much of how you feel. You're playing it safe—the way Hemingway did most of the time.

GORDON LISH: When Ken was writing *Sometimes a Great Notion* he was as impeccable a literary artist as there ever was. He changed his attitude toward writing when the book was finished. At one point he told me that he had taken so much out of himself in writing the book that he was even thinking of suicide.

I didn't know how to interpret any of that, whether that was just playful stuff or authentic speech, but he was completely washed out.

Also, I think he had gotten a little too pleased with himself, and was beginning to get the notion that he could do no wrong. He wasn't willing to edit, he wasn't willing to slice out of *Notion* what needed slicing out of it.

But in the actual writing of the book Kesey could not have been more devoted to the high principles that animated him. After the book was finished he tended to get soft. Getting soft in his case was thinking that every word that came out of his mouth must be carved in stone.

GURNEY NORMAN: I think Kesey found a new medium. He had worked within the literary traditions. He was a literary man and he remained a literary man until he was finished writing *Sometimes a Great Notion*. By this time, they had torn Perry Lane down. Ken had learned even more about drugs and had attracted his entourage, which he didn't have when I first knew him.

By 1963 there was money coming in from the books. And within a few weeks of Kesey's moving to La Honda, so many people from Perry Lane had gravitated to La Honda and were camped around there that it had become the new gathering scene.

My point is that the end of his writing career at that time and the taking on of this new artistic form, in which life itself is a novel, just segued very perfectly. You can't tell where one leaves off and the other begins. By the time *Notion* was published in 1964, Kesey was ready to make the declaration that he was through with writing.

KEN KESEY: ["The Neon Renaissance"] is a name I hooked onto a thing I feel is happening nowadays [1963]. What this is I cannot say exactly, except that it's a need to find a new way to look at the world, an attempt to locate a better reality, now that the old reality is riddled with radioactive poison. I think a lot of people are working in a lot of different ways to locate this reality—Ornette Coleman in jazz, Ann Halprin in dance, the New Wave in movies, Lenny Bruce in comedy, Wally Hendrix in art, Heller, Burroughs, Rechy, Gunter Grass in writing, and those thousands of others whose names would be meaningless, either because they haven't made IT yet, or aren't working in a medium that has as its end an IT to make. But all these people are trying to find out *what* is happening, *why*, and what can be *done* with it.

ROBERT STONE: I don't know if he really knew what his mission was. But I think he saw some kind of transition in America. These were tremendously optimistic times. America was at its apex of power and prosperity and I think Ken felt charged with this feeling.

Ken is not your average fellow. He was aware of his force, but not sure exactly what he was trying to do with it. He was also seeing the effect he was having on people and I think he was recognizing the lack of confidence on the part of many institutions. It was as if you went up to something and questioned it and it fell over. He was amazed at his own power and impressed with it. He was always basically a very decent guy, in that what he wanted to do was intended as a positive thing.

KEN KESEY: I get weary of people who use pessimism to avoid being responsible for all the problems in our culture. A man who says, "We're on the road to disaster," is seldom trying to wrench the wheel away from the driver. I prefer the troublemaker. He tells them he doesn't like the way they are running the show and, that he thinks he could do better. The fact is, he's going to try!

GORDON LISH: Kesey was a writer of impeccable discipline when I first knew him, a true champion, a true winner, a most admirable literary artist whose relations with the page were of the highest order.

But I think his heart was taken out of him when the New York establishment did not fall all over themselves on that book. I think Kesey wanted popular success too much. I think a lot of the whole gig that followed—the lunacy, the theater—was largely avoidance behavior. It was a way of not writing, even though some of it did have its merit.

ED MCCLANAHAN: I think there is probably some truth to the belief that Kesey felt rejected by New York after *Notion* was published. *Notion* hadn't been very well received, which was too bad. I think that to some extent reviewers felt that it was politically reactionary because it wasn't pro-union. The Goldwater campaign was going on, and Lyndon Johnson was so pro-union. I am sure to some extent he was suffering from bad reviews. Ken really is a writer, and in his heart he longed for those people to take him seriously.

KEN KESEY: I don't [write for posterity]. I'm writing for my brother, my dad, my mom, Faye, and the kids, the people I love and want to reach. Wait a minute. I'll add to that. I write for posterity in one kind of way that's hard to define. It's somewhere in something I remember from when I was a little kid. There was a stream that came down from the hill at our place and would have cut across our yard, but years before somebody went out there and covered this stream over with stone, mortared the stone together so that it left a hump down through the middle of this yard, as if it were left there by a 700-pound mole. And when the stream dried up my brother and I—he was in the third grade and I was in the fifth—we went down to the end of that tunnel and walked through it, lighting our way with torches. We found an old accordion under there. It was a great find, and we brought it home and tried to play it. But it wouldn't play, and we found out we could get into it by opening this screw and lifting the top off. We got into all the valves and bellows and everything, and there, stuck in a corner, we found a piece of paper, a sign, and it said, WHAT THE HELL YOU LOOKING IN HERE FOR, DAISY MAE? Well, I achieved some kind of satori right there—knowing that somebody had sometime, a very long while ago, gone in there and put that sign in that accordion, and he's betting all the time that someday somebody's going to come along and find it. A mystery for people to wonder about. Well, that's what I want for my books. . . .

. . .For one thing, I want to find out which side of me really is: the woodsy, logger side—complete with homespun homilies and crackerbarrel corniness, a valid side of me that I like—or its opposition. The two Stamper brothers in the novel are each one of the ways I think I am. . . . In college, for example, the guys on the wrestling team used to say, "You write? You act? What the hell you doing over with those people?" Over in the drama or writing department they were always bugging me about associating with a gang of thumpheads. Look, I don't intend to let anybody make me live in less world than I'm capable of living in. Babbs once said it perfectly: *A man should have the right to be as big as he feels it's in him to be.*

KEN KESEY'S BROTHER CHUCK (IN FOREGROUND) AND HIS COUSIN DALE KESEY IN LA HONDA. ACCORDING TO PRANKSTER RON BEVIRT, "THIS IS OREGONIAN TYPE OF FUN WHERE YOU PICK UP A CHUNK OF WOOD AND THROW IT, BASICALLY FOR ENTERTAINMENT." (RON BEVIRT)

THE MERRY PRANKSTERS HEAD TO MILLBROOK, NY TO MEET TIMOTHY LEARY AND THE MEMBERS OF HIS PSYCHEDELIC RESEARCH FOUNDATION. POET ALLEN GINSBERG JOINED THE PRANKSTERS IN NEW YORK CITY AND HELPED SET UP MEETINGS WITH JACK KEROUAC AND WITH LEARY, RAM DASS AND COMPANY. HIS PHOTOGRAPHS, TAKEN DURING THE TRIP TO MILLBROOK, APPEAR THROUGHOUT THIS SECTION. (ALLEN GINSBERG)

THE TRIP

"ON THE BUS"

(The first of a series of "on-board accounts" from the bus trip written by Ken Babbs. Using memory, imagination, and tapes from the Prankster archives, he offers an eyewitness comic-epic vision of events, people, and raps experienced "On the Bus.")

The timing was perfect. It was 1964. Goldwater was the Republican candidate for President, but America was emerging from the Eisenhower years. The Beatles wanted to hold your hand. The World's Fair was in Flushing Meadows, New York, for the 300th birthday of New York City. Patricia Neal and Melvyn Douglas won Oscars for Hud, *from Larry McMurtry's novel,* Horseman, Pass By. *The car had taken over as the major inroad on social behavior. Drive-in movies and darkened lanes . . . gropings of the unhooked bra, the upturned skirt, the outthrust thigh . . . moanings and pleadings and denials and promises and rings and pins exchanged . . . the reckless plunge . . . the space race gearing up . . . they were banging like rabbits . . . the arms race in full swing . . . drinking like fish . . . the brain-drain think tanks carving up the world . . . partying like the bomb was going to go off before they did . . . a growing involvement in Vietnam . . . college diplomas and gray flannel suits . . . the Cuban missile crisis . . . split-level homes . . . JFK's brains bloodspattered across Jackie's dress suit . . . color TV . . . freedom marchers murdered in Mississippi . . . gashog freeway cruisers . . . a caldron steaming around the edges . . . the fire is fueled by this innocent-looking bus . . . the lid is about to blow . . .*   —"The Intrepid Traveller"

(TOP) KEN BABBS: "1939 INTERNATIONAL HARVESTER SCHOOL BUS, FLATHEAD SIX, FIVE GEARS FORWARD, 10 X 20 SIX-PLY TIRES, DUALS ON THE REAR, CONVERTED INTO A CAMPER AND MODIFIED—PLATFORM ON REAR HOLDS MOTORCYCLE AND GENERATOR, LADDER AND TURRET TO FENCED-IN TOP FOR STORAGE AND VIEWING AND FILMING—FOR PRANKSTER USE." (BOTTOM) "BUS TANKING UP, PORT ARTHUR, TEXAS, THE BIG BUS SUCKS GAS, HOSE ABSOLUTELY CLEAN!" (RON BEVIRT)

"We hoped . . . [to] . . . stop the coming end of the world. . . ."

The bus trip began on June 14, 1964.

There were so many different agendas going into the bus trip that it's almost impossible to say exactly what it was *supposed* to be. The reality is that it became a metaphor for the carefree (and, at times, careless), hedonistic, authority-challenging, back-to-nature, alternative-seeking qualities of the 1960s. If there was one thing that Kesey and the Pranksters stood for, it was the power of individuals to stand up and be themselves, for each person to "be as big as he feels it's in him to be."

Twenty-five years after the bus trip, Kesey described its purpose to *Stanford Magazine* in terms no less grand than these: "What we hoped was that we could stop the coming end of the world."

In the unique fashion of the 1960s, the Pranksters' utopian idealism was almost always mixed with logic-eluding nonsense. Of course, this nonsense had its own purpose: When rationality is the tool of authority being irrational is a way to be free. It's also a way to avoid the rational expectations that inhibit spontaneity and creativity.

Kesey demonstrated this kind of thinking in an interview with Pacifica Radio in San Francisco in 1967, when he was asked to define what the Pranksters were doing.

Kesey: As navigator of this venture I try as much as possible to set out in a direction that, in the first place, is practically impossible to achieve, and then, along the way, mess up the minds of the crew with as many chemicals as we can lay our hands on, so it's almost certain that we can't get there.

Question: Well, would you say that it was deliberately self-defeating, then?

Kesey: This is about as deliberately self-defeating as anything has ever been in history. Most of the people, I think, involved in this realize that there's nothing to be gained.

This philosophy is a reflection of the methods Kesey brought to his own literary work. After *Cuckoo's Nest* was completed, he returned to Oregon where he worked as a logger to gather material for *Sometimes a Great Notion*. His approach to *Notion* was somewhat free-form, the way a jazz musician might start an interesting riff without necessarily knowing where he'll go with it. As he told an interviewer at a Palo Alto newspaper:

In *Cuckoo's Nest* I had the answer before I started. But with this latest book I didn't have the answer. Therefore, it was a good deal more painful, and cost a lot more sweat. I was struggling with myself as to whether I should continue on or quit. When I speak of quitting, I mean both living and writing. I contemplated suicide—only in the manner in which I toyed with insanity while writing the other book. But there are many forms of suicide.

The story itself is about a strong-minded family of loggers who decide to buck union strikers and keep logging. But the techniques Kesey used are experimental, in the masterful tradition of the works of a James Joyce or William Faulkner. Tenses change in mid-paragraph, as do points of view; yet these shifting perspectives (acid-inspired?) make for a more complete picture of the blustery world of the Stamper family. Using these techniques and weaving a story that didn't have a preconceived story line was a gigantic task, but the result was a book that some have called a masterpiece. As he told a Bay Area newspaper:

The book was difficult because its technique was completely new. I had no way of knowing when I was writing whether I was making any contact or not.

"I don't think I'll ever be able to do that again," Kesey recently told *Stanford Magazine*, referring to this method of writing.

After living the life of a literary monk, Kesey's agenda for the bus trip may have been partially to get some much-needed rest and relaxation. It may also have been to gather material for another book, or to pursue another medium, as many of his Stanford friends declared, and as the cameras and sound equipment hinted. Or maybe it was just to go see the World's Fair and attend his publication party for *Sometimes a Great Notion*. Whatever his reasons, he wasn't the only person directing the voyage.

Fourteen Pranksters, Fourteen Reasons for Going

Many of the other "Pranksters" took the trip just to get to the East. Jane ("Generally Famished") Burton, who was a neighbor of Kesey's and a member of the old Perry Lane gang, and Steve ("Zonker") Lambrecht were going to see friends in New York City. Paula ("Gretchen Fetchin") Sundsten was on her way to a waitressing job at a restaurant owned by the former

ROUTE OF THE MERRY PRANKSTERS' TRANSCONTINENTAL BUS TRIP

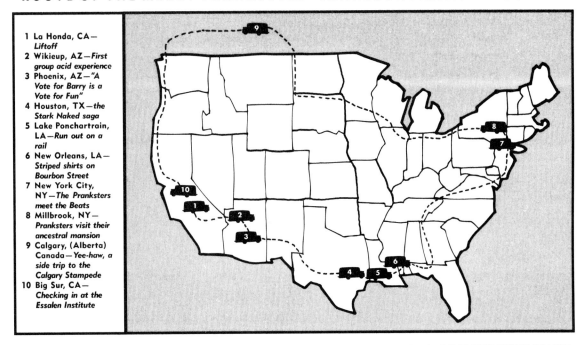

1 La Honda, CA—
   Liftoff
2 Wikieup, AZ—*First
   group acid experience*
3 Phoenix, AZ—*"A
   Vote for Barry is a
   Vote for Fun"*
4 Houston, TX—*the
   Stark Naked saga*
5 Lake Ponchartrain,
   LA—*Run out on a
   rail*
6 New Orleans, LA—
   *Striped shirts on
   Bourbon Street*
7 New York City,
   NY—*The Pranksters
   meet the Beats*
8 Millbrook, NY—
   *Pranksters visit their
   ancestral mansion*
9 Calgary, (Alberta)
   Canada—*Yee-haw, a
   side trip to the
   Calgary Stampede*
10 Big Sur, CA—
   *Checking in at the
   Essalen Institute*

IN THE COURSE OF THIS TRIP, THE PRANKSTERS SPENT $70,000 ON GASOLINE, ROAD FOOD AND MILES AND MILES OF 16-MILLIMETER FILM AND AUDIO-TAPE. APPROXIMATELY 45 HOURS OF FILM AND HUNDREDS OF HOURS OF AUDIO-TAPE RECORDED VIRTUALLY EVERY DRAMATIC ENCOUNTER, BABBLE, MOAN, AND ROAD SIGN OF THIS IMMORTAL TRIP. THE PURPOSE OF ALL THIS DOCUMENTATION WAS TO MAKE A MOVIE, *THE MERRY PRANKSTERS SEARCH FOR THE COOL PLACE.*

boxer Jack Dempsey. Both Gretchen and Zonker eventually stayed with the bus and returned to California.

Some of the Pranksters believed they were producing art from the beginning of the trip—*spontaneous* art of the let-it-happen-and-see-what-develops-on-the-film school of artistic expression. These were the hardcore Pranksters, who included Ken ("The Intrepid Traveller") Babbs, who had just gotten out of the Marine Corps after a stint as a helicopter pilot in Vietnam; Sandy ("Dis-mount") Lehmann-Haupt; George ("Hardly Visible") Walker; Mike ("Mal Function") Hagen, a frat brother of Kesey's from the University of Oregon; Ron ("Hassler") Bevirt who, fresh from a tour of duty in the Army, was along to try his hand at still photography; and Kathy Casano, who later earned the name "Stark Naked," came along because Hagen offered to make her a movie star. They believed in the trip's artistic possibilities. Also on board were Ken's brother Chuck ("Brother Charlie") and his cousin Dale ("Highly Charged") Kesey, along with Babbs's brother John ("Sometimes Missing"), who were basically on the bus to tour the country and ride with friends.

(TOP LEFT) FAYE AND KEN KESEY ON THE BUS AS THE PRANKSTERS PREPARE TO LEAVE FROM LA HONDA. (TOP AND BOTTOM RIGHT) BUS INTERIOR WITH ZONKER, KESEY, AND ROY SEBERN TESTING THE ON-BOARD SOUND SYSTEM. (BOTTOM LEFT) PAULA SUNDSTEN—

And then, of course, there was Neal Cassady ("Sir Speed Limit"), who came along just a few days before the trip started. He approached the task of driving as a professional, but it was a job he was uniquely suited for and he no doubt enjoyed it. He was an instinctual driver with the uncanny ability to stay up almost continuously and talk constantly while he did it.

All told, there were fourteen people on the bus who became known as the Merry Band of Pranksters. They spent $70,000 (most of it Kesey's money from book advances and movie rights) buying gasoline, road food ("ratburgers," according to Ken Babbs), and miles and miles of 16-millimeter film and audio-tape. Approximately fifty hours of film and hundreds of hours of audio-tape recorded virtually every dramatic encounter, babble, moan, and road sign of this immortal trip. The purpose of all this documentation was to make a movie, *The Merry Pranksters Search for the Cool Place.*

The Movie

What has come of it, since the trip 25 years ago, is a still-massive work-in-progress. Despite weeks, months, some say *years* of attempts to make sense of it all by Kesey, Ken Babbs, and others (including Hollywood producers), *The Merry Pranksters Search for the Cool Place* hasn't yet been edited into a theatrical release, though parts of it have appeared in the lectures-shows given by Ken Babbs, who speculates that its future may lie in video.

Of course, no one knew these things at the time. They simply did the best they could to record the scenes of the trip: Neal Cassady driving the bus across Texas, the camera trained on his handsome face as he smoked a joint, made faces, and rapped continuously—*all at the same time!* Kesey on top of the bus in Alabama, playing the flute with an American flag wrapped around his head like Captain America. Gretch buying ratburgers in the Deep South. Babbs "performing surgery" with gin and tampons on a festering bug bite on Hagen's leg. And the whole bunch of them welcoming a teenaged runaway on board, who strips to her skivvies as the Pranksters paint her nubile body the colors of the magic bus.

They *filmed, filmed, filmed* all across America, nine stops in all: from California through Arizona; through Texas; through Louisiana; through parts of Florida, before making a left turn and heading up to New York to see Cassady's old buddy Jack Kerouac and the media's LSD gurus Timothy Leary and Richard Alpert. They did finally attend the New York World's Fair.

With this film the Pranksters set about, as one of their tribal songs went, to "change the course of time"—and perhaps someday earn some pranking capital.

As the Pranksters' legend grew, this cross-country voyage gained a mythical status. But as in other myths—Homer's *Odyssey*, or, closer to home, Kerouac's *On the Road*— it's easy to overlook that the voyage itself was a string of days and nights of grinding intercontinental travel in an antiquated bus.

"You have to realize," says Ron Bevirt, "that this was an unpleasant trip. It was noisy and chaotic on the bus. Some people wanted to be left alone and others wanted to keep sticking a camera in everyone's face. On top of that, it was hot. This was summer and we were going through the South. We couldn't get cool. We couldn't stop sweating. At times we couldn't hear anything but the noise of the bus. [But] the most memorable experiences are often the most unpleasant ones."

It was only later that people realized that the bus trip was the beginning of a cultural myth. From the trip came the slogan "You're either on the bus or off the bus." Implying, of course, that it's hip to be "on." But no one knew at the time exactly how hip it might someday seem to have been on the bus. There was no massive youth culture to lead. Even the Beatles hadn't hit yet. The closest thing to tribal anthems these guys had came from the Weavers!

FOOTAGE FROM THE 45-HOUR CINEMATIC MONOLITH *THE MERRY PRANKSTERS SEARCH FOR THE COOL PLACE*. (PRANKSTER ARCHIVES)

THE TRIP: ORAL HISTORIES . . .

. . . in which Kesey, frustrated with the limitations of his career as a popular novelist, initiates a communal adventure involving the formation of a group, which: purchases a school bus; paints it a variety of colors by spraying, brushing, smearing, and walking on the roof; and equips it with movie cameras, tape recorders, amplified sound systems, musical instruments, costumes, American flags, and a supply of LSD. . . .

The adventurers dub themselves "The Merry Pranksters" and undertake a cross-country trip from La Honda, California, to New York City. The Pranksters seek "a cool place" and make stops to film, see the country, have their countrymen see them, tootle on musical instruments while floating in inner tubes, and trip together on LSD. With Neal Cassady at the wheel, they ride through: Wikieup, Arizona; Phoenix, Arizona; Houston, Texas; New Orleans, Louisiana; and along the highway through Mississippi, Alabama, Florida, Georgia, and Tennessee, before heading north to New York City. In Manhattan, they attend a party with writers Jack Kerouac and Allen Ginsberg, and the next day drive to Millbrook, New York, for a meeting with Timothy Leary and his followers at the Castalia Foundation. . . .

On the completion of this journey, the Pranksters decide to carry on their explorations back home in California, and find themselves among the grand marshals of a suddenly burgeoning, bi-coastal, psychedelic parade.

This section features commentary from:
Robert Stone, Ken Babbs, Ron Bevirt, Ken Kesey, Ed McClanahan, and:
KEN KESEY—a.k.a. the "Chief" and "Swashbuckler," in comments from a 1965 address to teachers of writing, sponsored by the National Defense Educators Act, and also from Prankster archival material compiled by Ken Babbs.
LEE QUARNSTROM—the "Minister of Information" for the Pranksters, now a reporter and columnist for the *San Jose Mercury News*.
STEVE LAMBRECHT—a.k.a. "Zonker" of the Merry Pranksters
ALLEN GINSBERG—poet and photographer, currently Distinguished Professor of English at Brooklyn College in New York and Director Emeritus of the Jack Kerouac School of Disembodied Poetics at Naropa Institute in Boulder, Colorado.
TIMOTHY LEARY—Harvard University clinical psychologist

turned explorer-advocate of LSD, he is now an author, lecturer, and designer of interactive computer software.

B A B A R A M D A S S —in 1964, known as Richard Alpert, a colleague of Timothy Leary's at Harvard interested in the study of LSD as a means to attain enlightenment, currently a writer and lecturer.

REAR VIEW OF THE BUS PARKED ALONG A ROAD'S SHOULDER. KEN BABBS: "EVERY TIME THE BUS LURCHED, A PIECE OF IT FELL AND KNOCKED OFF A BUNCH OF SOUND GEAR. ALL THE TAPE RECORDERS WERE PILED ON THE SINK—AN ELECTRICAL CALAMITY." (RON BEVIRT)

" K E N   K E S E Y — ' T H E   C H I E F ' "

KESEY AS CAPTAIN FLAG. KEN BABBS DESCRIBES THE SCENE: "CAPTAIN FLAG, PLAYED BY KEN KESEY, PREPARES TO MOUNT THE REAR PLATFORM AND EXHORT MOTORISTS ON THE NEW JERSEY TURNPIKE TO 'SALUTE, DAMMIT, SALUTE!'" (RON BEVIRT)

esey didn't graduate from college in anything as staid as English. He was a Performing Arts major, did a Lord Buckley imitation for his Graduation Recital: "Mark a golden spike where that cat blew!"

He'll stock up the bus and take it and the Pranksters to New York, tripping all the way. The parts the Pranksters play will be both as assumed characters and as real persons showing themselves in real life, a la documentaire, much like the settlers of 1894 coming across the Great Plains.

Captain Marvel, Captain America, Davy Crockett, Lord Buckley, J.P. Barnum, Paul Revere, John Wayne, Casey Jones, Carl Sandburg, John Henry, Hank Stamper, Herman Melville, Paul Bunyan, Randle Patrick McMurphy; bulls-eye marble shooting champ, baby coon capturer, cave explorer, flesh-eater, blood-guzzler, dead shot (Rifle to shoulder he aims in at a raccoon in a tree. The raccoon says, "Is your name KEN KESEY?! I thought so. You needn't take no further trouble," and he hikes down the tree, for he already considers himself shot, but Kesey pats him on the head and says, "I hope I shoot myself first for I've never had such a compliment in my life."), champeen wrassler, argufier, lover, elocutioner, writer, actor, owner of the ugliest dog in the West; runs faster, dives deeper, stays under longer and comes out higher than any man on the McKenzie; outscreams a panther, outstares a flash of lightning, totes a Nash Rambler on his back, plays rough and tumble with a mountain lion, sleeps under a blanket of snow; walks like an ox, runs like a fox, swims like an eel, yells like a banshee, fights like a devil, spouts like an earthquake, makes love like a mad bull, and swallows a bear whole without choking if someone butters the critter's head and pins back its ears; he's also the author of the best-selling novel, One Flew Over the Cuckoo's Nest, *and he has to be in New York City in two weeks for the publication party of his new book,* Sometimes a Great Notion.

He moves into the hills between Stanford and the ocean under huge redwoods—a log cabin, creek between road and property, a Ron Boise welded statue gate, and a continuation of the weekend LSD gobblings when a whole new innovation is added: Movies! *Buy a bus, stock her up and take the show on the road, filming and taping and tripping all the way.*

"The unsettlers of 1964 going backwards across the Great Plains," Kesey says. "All of these things have a mythic story. . . ."

—"The Intrepid Traveller"

"THE INTREPID TRAVELLER PRESENTS THE LEGEND OF THE INTREPID TRAVELLER"

One night before the bus was born, before the bus was even considered, The Intrepid Traveller was born.

A young man comes trooping down the hill.

The young man was born in the same town as James Thurber and was kissed on the cheek by the Governor of Ohio. He grew up on the shores of Lake Erie and was the Dad's Club scholar-athlete of the year. He attended Miami University in Oxford, Ohio, "the cradle of coaches," and got trounced regularly in handball by Ara Parseghian. He shot clay pigeons with Walter ("Smokey") Alston and sat at the same table with Weeb

KEN BABBS AND NEAL CASSADY PILOTING THE BUS TOWARD MILLBROOK. (ALLEN GINSBERG)

Ewbank. He graduated with honors in English and was on the basketball team that went to two NCAA tournaments. He held Oscar Robertson to 46 points and got flattened by Jerry West on a breakaway lay-up. His teammate was Wayne Embry, who played for the Cincinnati Royals and the Boston Celtics and who is now the general manager of the Cleveland Cavaliers. He met Bill Russell. He was in the Stanford writing class with Ken Kesey, Wendell Berry, Ernie Gaines, and Mitch Strucinski. He was a Marine pilot and flew helicopters in Vietnam. He was on the bus. He rode an elevator with Jimmy Breslin. He passed the Acid Test. He partied with Hunter S. Thompson and the Hell's Angels. He was written up by Tom Wolfe. He drove the Bam Truck from Mexico and got Bob Stone a ticket. He gigged with the Grateful Dead more times than they'd care to remember. He was mentioned by Gurney Norman in Divine

Right's Trip. *He camped out for a summer in the Truchas Peaks with Wavy Gravy and the Hog Farm. He shook Ravi Shankar's hand, soft as a butterfly's wing. He was kissed on the cheek by Joàn Baez at Woodstock. Johnny Winters and B.B. King did a show on his free stage at the Texas Pop Festival. He had lunch with Larry McMurtry. He played poker with Ed McClanahan. He's written for* Rolling Stone, Running *magazine,* Oregon Magazine, Eugene Magazine, Esquire, *and* American Health. *He spent an evening with Norman Mailer. He was co-founder and editor of* Spit In the Ocean, *a revolving poker-hand publication. He met Andy Warhol and Kurt Vonnegut at Elaine's. He published and edited* The Bugle—*"it blows what it knows and knows what it blows." He drove Roy Blount to the La Guardia Airport. He was editor of* The Bend in the River Reality, *the originator of the media referendum. He worked with Rahsaan Roland Kirk at the ITSART Hoohaw. He's done readings with Bob Kaufman and Jack Michelline, got drunk with L'enfant Terrible, been photographed by Robert Frank, played pool with Paul Newman, shook hands with the commandant of the Marine Corps, got kicked off the stage by Bill Graham's goons, stuck his finger in Paul Krassner's chicken pot pie, did a gig with Bill Murray, and exchanged mutterings with Jack Kerouac. He's collaborating with Ken Kesey on a novel about the Pendleton Roundup. He's participated in workshops with Timothy Leary, William S. Burroughs, Anne Waldman, and Lawrence Ferlinghetti. He was player-coach for the Springfield Creamery Jugs, Industrial League champs three years running. He was kissed on the cheek by Allen Ginsberg. His wife waited on Joe Namath at Hamburger Henry's. He's writing a war novel. He picked up Bill Walton's watch crystal—"Uh, you dropped your contact, Bill." He lives with his wife and kids in the foothills of the Cascades, and from there, in the bosom of his home, he cranks out his merry and varied works.*

Another young man, Hagen, asks the first young man, "Who are you and where goest thou?"

"I. I am The Intrepid Traveller. I cross yon plain."

"Oh, you are an Intrepid Traveller indeed to attempt to cross such a vast plain."

In the background, the sound of tom-toms beating.

"Yea," sayest The Intrepid Traveller, "and some day I will take my whole band across the great plain."

And verily they did buy one bus and crossed. . . .   —"The Intrepid Traveller"

ED McCLANAHAN: After putting out two enormous novels in a few years, [Kesey] was really ready to explore some different mediums. I think he really felt somehow or another that writing fiction—and, if you look back on it, not very conventional fiction—was constraining and he needed to break out of it. I think the bus trip was an attempt to make living art.

The reviews for *Sometimes a Great Notion* were generally less laudatory than those for *One Flew Over the Cuckoo's Nest*. Reviewers noted the massive effort that Kesey sustained in bringing together myriad themes, characters, and perspectives, but differed in their assessments of how well this task was accomplished. The *New York Times* noted "the power and scope" of the novel, and the reviewer called it "a big book in every way, [capturing] the tenor of post-Korea America as nothing I can remember reading." However, the headline of the *Newsweek* review was "Lumbering" and noted that "Kesey's book, for all his intensity of purpose, attempts to be all-inclusive and ends up elephantine."

KEN KESEY: First, let me make it understood I am not a writer. I haven't written anything since I wrote those last drafts of *Notion* and I don't intend to write anything else. I have many reasons for this, the main one being that to continue writing would mean that I couldn't continue my work.

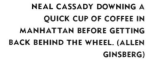

NEAL CASSADY DOWNING A QUICK CUP OF COFFEE IN MANHATTAN BEFORE GETTING BACK BEHIND THE WHEEL. (ALLEN GINSBERG)

LEE QUARNSTROM: One of the best things about being a Prankster was that there were these two people—Neal and Kesey—who all on their own were worth throwing in your lot with. I mean, I would have thrown in my lot with Neal without Kesey or with Kesey without Neal. But having them both together was like, wow!

KEN KESEY: [As a novelist] you learn to do a thing, you get to where you can do it with so much ease and cleverness, and then you begin to do it over and over again. You find that there's a market for it and a demand for it and a lot of times there is more demand for it than you realize; there's a kind of panic demand. "Hell, I can knock out a novel for *Esquire,* serialize it and do it in six months. Then get back to my serious work."

I don't think you should ever do that. Once you start writing commercials and sell into it, then that's it.

So, I have been devoting myself to a lot more serious work, like riding around on buses and exploring the insides of various jail houses.

RON BEVIRT: I don't know that there was any real concrete plan for making some kind of documentary about the World's Fair. The filming was all kind of connected to some of our evolved philosophy, which was simply trying to "be in the now." We were trying to be spontaneous and record things as they spontaneously occurred.

GEORGE WALKER WITH MOVIE CAMERA, FILMING THE PRANKSTER MOVIE NEAR NEW YORK CITY'S CENTRAL PARK. KEN BABBS REMEMBERS THAT HE WAS ABOUT TO FILM VIKING PRESS SECRETARIES AS THEY BOARDED THE BUS FOR A RIDE. (RON BEVIRT)

There had been various discussions along the way about the pros and cons of trying to script out the action in some way, even block out some action to occur in the film. That had been rejected in favor of just totally being spontaneous in filming and recording things as they occurred. So that is pretty much what was going on. But even that wasn't done perfectly because there were lots of times when nobody was recording or filming when significant things were going on. It was kind of haphazard and chaotic. It was all much like real life.

KEN KESEY: I went back and looked at *Cuckoo's Nest* some time ago and to my surprise, as much as I still feel for the book and the situation, I recognize it as a very elaborate commercial, an advertisement, that if I remove my personal likes and dislikes about what I see in the world, it's this: It's a thing that comes in like the Bayer aspirin pain ad that says "pain, pain, pain." It sells you what I think is a particular pain in the world, then goes on to sell you what I think is the particular alleviation for that pain.

I have no idea whether or not it is true. I wasn't there; I made it up. I designed, almost before I thought of it, little map points in my head that we call plots, that I was seeing in front of me, and then I took the life I was seeing out in front of me to go along meticulously and make all of those points. This is what almost all of our literature is doing; this is what almost all of our movies and television plays are doing right now. They take the particular axe that the writer has to grind and then the particular adroitness with which he conceals the grinding is how you judge his ability as a writer.

RON BEVIRT: After writing *Notion* he was ready to kick back for a while. And *Notion* was going to be coming out in New York and he had to go to New York for the appearance of the book in 1964. He and George Walker and a few others thought they could throw a mattress into the back of the panel truck and go to New York for the World's Fair.

Babbs was finishing up his time in the service at El Toro Marine Base, so they planned to pick him up. Then the number of people involved kind of grew. Finally, Kesey decided that he needed more than a panel truck for this number. That is when he and George shopped around and found the bus.

KEN KESEY: I found that no matter how hard I tried to find new areas of my mind or another person's mind in my writing, I would be walking through territory and see that there is Shakespeare's sign. He did it, and we've been doing it over and over again. He set a standard and everything since then has been redoing the same thing, with just changing the plots and the emotional play just a little bit. I found that I couldn't sit down to write without forming this perfect little birthday cake to sell to people.

So I started going out and taping with tape recorders and filming, and going back to look over what I had filmed and taped to see if people talked like they did in novels, and they don't. A tape-recorded conversation doesn't look like anything you read. A moment-to-moment account of what goes on doesn't look like any novel that you come across.

ED MCCLANAHAN: [While preparing the bus for the trip,] everybody was getting bombed more and more and there was just more going on

PAINTER AND PRANKSTER ROY SEBERN WAS AMONG THE FIRST TO PAINT THE BUS, AND HE PROVIDED ITS NAME— "FURTHUR," WHICH AT VARIOUS TIMES ALSO APPEARED ON THE BUS'S DESTINATION SIGN AS "FURTHER." (RON BEVIRT)

and they started painting it up. That started getting wilder and wilder, and the first thing you know more and more people were kind of signing on. I don't think he planned anything that the group ended up doing. . . .

I'll bet you wouldn't be too far off to say that when he bought that bus he thought of it more or less the same way that people think of RVs, that it was going to be his kind of camper, and that he would take a group. And I imagine that he was just thinking that most of them would be family and that they would go to the World's Fair. But as a friend said about Kesey, "He is wildly gregarious and once he starts something like that more and more people get into it, and it gets bigger than he planned."

I think that is what happened later with the Acid Tests. They were just parties up in La Honda to begin with, and then they started having them in other places. Then the Grateful Dead [known until late 1965 as the Warlocks] started showing up; then Hell's Angels started coming; then the FBI. . . .

KEN KESEY: I haven't been reading a whole hell of a lot, to tell you the truth. I feel as though if I looked back on this period in 500 years I wouldn't look at the literature to see what was going on. I'd listen to the rock and roll music, I'd go to the movies, I'd read the comic books. You read literature here you might get a good idea of what was going on 150 years ago, but not right now. Painting, sculpture, and music are breaking out of their bonds. Writing has remained the same for a god-awful long time.

RON BEVIRT: We were bored with the grayness and nothingness of life. We were hungry for change. In the bus trip we were working at being spontaneous. And we were working at having fun. We were really having fun! And we were Pranksters. We were a Merry Band of Pranksters!

KEN BABBS: We were the Astronauts of Inner Space, which is as big as outer space. As above so below. We popped acid, flopped on the floor, hooked up tape recorders, and rapped out whole novels. We got up on our feet and played musical instruments, acting out parts we made up on the spot. This wasn't a summer lark, but a legitimate literary endeavor of artistic merit, holding the promise of commercial success.

JOHN BABBS, KEN'S BROTHER, A COLLEGE ENGLISH TEACHER ON SUMMER VACATION. (RON BEVIRT)

"LIFTOFF"

The crossing could not be made on foot, a twentieth-century mode was needed. They were taking back painting from the painters, releasing the artist within. Providing exactly what the bus needed—bright colors to gussy her up a bit. Movie cameras are added. They'll take the cameras and the tape recorders on the bus and film and tape the whole trip.

The bus is parked in the drive of Kesey's house in La Honda, California. Once a plodding workhorse school bus carrying 1939 end-of-depression scrubbed-fresh schoolyard kids, the rig seemingly has the dimensions of an aircraft carrier. Three tiers of bunks line the sides of the back third. The mid-third consists of a dining suite bolted to the floor, along with a complete kitchen. The front third is the navigation compartment—with map rack, two-way radio, CB, and short wave. The cockpit and enormous driver's console take up the area behind the dash and windshield.

"She's a beaut, isn't she?" Kesey says. "A 1939 International. Perfect rig for taking to Manhattan, room for the whole merry band."

Attracted by the sound of John Coltrane blasting out of the speakers sitting in the yard, Janet, a fifteen-year-old neighbor girl comes over to see what is happening. As soon as she hears the word "paint," she sticks her bare foot into a tray of green paint and climbs up on the bus and walks across the roof. Roy Sebern dips his thumb into a can of yellow and climbs up on the hood.

"What this old bus needs is a good luck name to help keep it from breaking down," Roy says. "A word that, with whatever power words have, contributes that power toward the bus making it to New York. It should be a poem too, like a poet makes a poem and puts it out in the world, only short. A haiku is fewer words than most poems, and one word is even fewer words than that, so this one lucky word is what she'll have for a name."

"FURTHUR," he paints on the signboard above the windshield. . . .

—"The Intrepid Traveller"

FURTHUR BUS STOPPED FOR GAS NEAR POUGHKEEPSIE, N.Y. ON THE ROAD TO MILLBROOK. (ALLEN GINSBERG)

SCULPTOR RON BOISE, A
NEIGHBOR OF KESEY'S IN LA
HONDA, WHO ASSISTED ON
MODIFICATIONS OF THE BUS. KEN
BABBS DESCRIBES SOME OF THE
PIECES OF OUTDOOR SCULPTURE
BOISE HAD BEEN WORKING ON AT
THAT TIME: "[HE] CONVERTED
CAR BODIES INTO KAMASUTRA
BODIES AND MADE THEIR ORGANS
TWANG TO THE TOUCH."
(RON BEVIRT)

STEVE LAMBRECHT: I don't know how the whole bus trip got started. I was just a hitchhiker. My girlfriend had one of those guest editorships at *Mademoiselle* magazine in the summer of 1964 and I was going to go back there and meet her and screw around on the East Coast a while.

KEN KESEY: The painting took place over two or three days. We started kind of slow and were still painting it the day we left. Someone took an old broom up on the top and spilled some paint and wiped around with the broom, making patterns. People walked around in bare feet on the bus, leaving footprints of paint. We poured some paint on it and drove it so it would streak back and give it kind of a flame-hooded appearance. We drove four miles down the road and ran out of gas.

Then, before we finished painting it, Hagen took it over. He had this fantasy, I just couldn't understand it, talked and talked about it, about putting something on top of it. I argued and argued with him about it, saying there are more important things to get done than a turret. Besides, I didn't like the idea of people on top of that bus, anyway.

ED MCCLANAHAN: I remember Ken building a kind of deck on the back of the bus. They started out with a barber chair out on the back so you could sit there and admire the passing scenery. Ken was underneath the bus hammering down there and he crawled out and said, "McClanahan, I have to remind myself these days that I'm not a goddamn carpenter, I'm a writer."

KEN KESEY: I've thought about Hagen's fantasy a whole lot of times. Every time he gets a wild fantasy I don't understand, my natural inclination is to say "no." But often I get great benefit out of those fantasies.

KEN BABBS: The need to paint the bus? It all came from this thing about "taking painting back from the painters," just like we were taking writing back from the writers. Anybody can do this stuff, you just have to have the freedom to do it however you want. America really represents freedom. Also, this bus needed some bright colors.

STEVE LAMBRECHT: I had friends who had taken acid, but up to this point I had only been smoking pot. I took some about a month before starting on the bus trip. We did it up behind Kesey's place at La Honda. This comes back in fragments, but I remember that I was up there tripping-out on the trees and then I became conscious that I was actually humping a tree! I must have thought that the tree was some kind of vestal virgin in a primeval forest. I can remember realizing what folly that was.

Anyway, heading back down into camp I found a bunch of the Pranksters tying foam rubber to their feet, using them as sandals. I did it too and ended up in a creek. They don't work well in a creek because they get soggy.

But at any rate, that was my introduction to getting high.

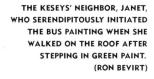

THE KESEYS' NEIGHBOR, JANET, WHO SERENDIPITOUSLY INITIATED THE BUS PAINTING WHEN SHE WALKED ON THE ROOF AFTER STEPPING IN GREEN PAINT. (RON BEVIRT)

"WHY'D HE TAKE THAT TRIP, ANYWAY?"

tire squealed and a two-tone, pink and purple Dodge, riding low on tortured shocks and spurting smoke with every change of the accelerator, raced into the curve and skidded across the bridge.

Dust settled in the driveway. The radio blared "Love Potion Number Nine."

"It was eight to five on your making it over that bridge," Kesey yelled.

"Pshaw," Neal Cassady snorted. "Nothing to it."

He took a big swig from a can of beer. His veins stood out like hemp rope. Chest bulging beneath a frayed blue polo shirt. His jeans hung below his belly. Smoke blew out his nose. He ground a Camel under his heel.

"Then it's Sunday morning next week as I understand it that you want me in a movie?" he said, walking up to Kesey. "Be gone two weeks? If you could loan me one hundred bucks, I'll send it off to Carolyn and I won't need any money because I'll be living on you from Sunday on, isn't that right? Until we get to New York? Easily within the limit of the two weeks my boss will give me. Funny, I've done this every summer since I was fifteen. I go on a trip with a car. And this is the first time I realized it."

"Then why don't you stay up here and take some of this LSD and spend the rest of the day with the people who will probably be present on this bus trip?" Kesey asked him.

"Right," Cassady said. "And orient my vibrations around them."

"You got it," Kesey said.

—"The Intrepid Traveller"

NEAL CASSADY OUTSIDE A DINER IN THE SOUTH. LEE QUARNSTROM REMEMBERS AN EPISODE OF CASSADY'S DRIVING PROWESS: "SOMEHOW BY COAXING THIS CAR—THROWING IT INTO GEAR, THROWING IT OUT OF GEAR, COASTING A LONG WAYS—WE FINALLY ROLLED TO A DEAD STOP TWO MILES LATER IN FRONT OF A GAS PUMP ON EL CAMINO REAL. THAT WAS TYPICAL OF HIS WIZARDRY BEHIND THE WHEEL." (RON BEVIRT)

STEVE LAMBRECHT: Cassady and I had bumped into each other years and years before the bus trip, when I was about twelve or fourteen years old. He was changing tires in a truck tire shop right next to my dad's place in San Jose. I used to take my bike down the alley and watch these guys change tires. I can remember very specifically one day sitting there, drinking a Nehi orange drink, and listening to three guys who talked about this fellow who did the work of three men. And I sat there and watched him, throwing tire sledge hammers around, wearing coveralls and acting all wired-up. I just never realized it until after the bus trip was over and Cassady's wife Carolyn told me that he used to work in that truck tire shop.

ED McCLANAHAN: I decided not to go. The bus looked like a bust waiting to happen. We had two kids and I thought that there was the likelihood that everybody was going to come back in irons. I now think somebody was watching over them, I'll tell you that.

KEN BABBS: We were using America as the set, and the people of America as part of the experience and drama that would happen. We had no idea how it would turn out. There were countless surprises and we were lucky enough to capture some good ones. For instance, the morning after we left Los Angeles Jane Burton woke up to a big surprise.

The bus is parked by the Big Sandy River near Wikieup, Arizona, stuck in the sand. Cassady, shirtless and sweating, is strutting back and forth.

NEAL CASSADY SEEN IN THE REARVIEW MIRROR OF THE BUS. (RON BEVIRT)

"**E N R O U T E**"

Jane Burton was counting on the bus getting her to New York in time to visit with a friend who was about to go overseas. On this bus it looked like they were not going to provide safety pins or Kotexes. It looked at first like it was every woman for herself. . . .

"**I**'ve tried, you know, to make a form *of saying we're being handled by a higher power*," Neal Cassady is telling Jane. "You have to use the same body you begin the symphony with, y'see? But that's the thing—group experience. What is there but One Force? That is, of the soul? And with judicious application of that One Force can't one go to the higher, mmmm, fourth plane *riches? Mmmm?*"

"I'm not interested, Cassady," Jane Burton says. "You know why I'm not interested? Last night, when I was sleeping in one of the upper bunks, my purse slipped down between the bunk and the bus and fell out the open window and I lost everything. A few hundred dollars worth of traveller's checks, all my cash, my I.D., and my driver's license. Everything I didn't want to lose I had put in my purse. I could have lost my suitcase easily. Here I am, pregnant—oh shit, don't tell anyone I said that—and now, on top of everything else, I don't have a dime."

"You need the blindness to have the light," Cassady says. "Chance is chance and chance is chance but how many far-looking chances do you have to have thrown in your face to find out it's all 400 percent chance? Mmmm?"

"You may be right, but I was trapped and I was feeling awful and then I realized I had to brush my teeth and my toothbrush was in my purse. Everybody here is so stoned it's impossible to communicate my problem. I'd like to go up to someone and say, 'I really want to borrow your toothbrush but I know that you probably won't want to loan me your toothbrush, am I right?' and that person is bound to say, 'Yeah, you're right,' so what am I going to do?"

"I don't mind if you want to use my toothbrush," Cassady says.

"Really, Neal? Can I borrow your toothbrush?"

"Well, certainly, ma'am. You certainly can and here it is."

He brings out the toothbrush. It's wrapped in a clean, white handkerchief.

"I'd be very proud to loan it to you," he says. "And it's never been used!"

— "The Intrepid Traveller"

STEVE LAMBRECHT: We didn't really dip into the acid until Wikieup. That was when they spray-painted my T-shirt and then made me put it on and I got paint all over my back.

Then, of course, I can remember Neal playing the guitar. I should say "trying" to play the guitar. They have these pictures of him looking so happy while he's strumming but it didn't sound so good, I can tell you that. All these people were doing this crazy shit and I just laid back and watched.

Shortly after drinking from the communal bottle of acidified orange juice near a lake outside Wikieup, Arizona, Paula Sundsten's delighted wonder at the magnificence of sunlit algae resulted in her being known forever after as "Gretchen Fetchin the Slime Queen." Also in Wikieup Kathy Casano did a star turn for the cameras. But it wasn't until the Pranksters reached Houston that she would receive her prankster name—"Stark Naked."

PAULA SUNDSTEN DIVES INTO WATER IN WIKIEUP, ARIZONA AND EMERGES COVERED WITH ALGAE AND MUD, ECSTATICALLY TRANSFORMED INTO GRETCHEN FETCHIN, THE SLIME QUEEN. (RON BEVIRT)

"THE LEGEND OF STARK NAKED"

Hagen wanted to bring along a girl named Kathy. No one knew her and there was some concern. These astronauts of inner space were as highly specialized as those of outer space, and to take along someone they didn't know filled them with trepidation. She was naked—Stark Naked.

Chapter 1—The Wikieup Debacle

"Oh, let me buy the food," Kathy says. "I haven't been of any help so far."

"You?" Babbs says. "Well, why not? But make it snappy. We'll be gassed up and out of here in a few minutes. Here's a twenty. That oughta cover it."

"Good for you, Babbs," Hagen says. "First friendly thing I've seen anyone do with her since we left."

"Aw, shucks. Us gyrenes ain't all bulldog breath and leather neck. Mine's sweaty. It's hot out here in this desert."

"Must be a cool place somewhere," Hassler says. "Even desert rats need water."

"Water!" Zonk yells. "Cool, clear water. My body is aching to wallow in water."

"Anything to take my mind off food," Hassler says.

Chapter 2—She Returns

"Oyster crackers get stale very fast in this humidity. Or, sorely. So we'll swallow it. Let it melt in the heat," Cassady says.

"Hey," Hagen says to the grumbling crew. "Lighten up." He turns to Kathy. "It's OK, they don't mean anything, just yakking, you know how they are."

"I don't know anything. I've been kicking myself in the ass ever since we left for coming on this trip. I can't do anything right."

"Well, you got to admit, one limp little lobster tail and a small box of stale oyster crackers doesn't really cut it for this crew," Hagen says to her.

"I noticed they gulped down those crackers fast enough! Then dumped the lobster tail in that filthy sink. No wonder no one will touch it!" Kathy says.

"It's the mind, working all the time, though it's not a question of work," Cassady

yells. "It's a pleasure, a quirk, a schematical misunderstanding. Its negativity is ticking out, the same thing as oysters in Prescott: oyster crackers of course."

"Ratburgers! That's all we get to eat on this bus," Kathy mutters. "Most cheap-o kind of hamburger you can buy. Anything under 24 cents. Hideous!"

"OK, Pranksters, muster up," Kesey says. "We'll have a brief briefing before we alight. Pass the orange juice around while I describe what we'll try to do. Hagen will be on the Arriflex. George on the Bolex. Hassler on the still camera. Sandy, run the microphones out as far as they will go. You four guys go easy on the acid. This time, me and Babbs and Zonk and John and Dale and Chuck and Paula and Kathy and Jane will be the loaded loonies, out for a cool place lark. Next time we'll trade off. That way we'll be sure to get some good stuff."

"I'll pass on dropping the acid," Jane says. "I'll be the assistant, or whatever it's called in the big-time movie business."

KATHY CASANO, A.K.A "STARK NAKED." KEN BABBS:
"WEARING ONLY A BRA AND PANTIES, KATHY DIVES
HEADFIRST INTO A CLUMP OF FLOWERS. . . . 'SUCH BEAUTY . . .
JUST LIKE A LITTLE BABY,' SHE CRIES, ROLLING IN THE CLUMP.
THEN SHE BEGINS TO SCREAM." (RON BEVIRT)

"This is the big time," Kesey says. *"It doesn't get any bigger than this. Let's start loading the film magazines and—hey! Whoa up there, Kathy! I said only a slug, not half the bottle."*

"Half the bottle, hell," George says. *"She drank the whole damn thing!"*

Chapter 3—Stark Naked

"What about a piss stop?" Dale wants to know.

"Piss stop, aye," Cassady says. *"First cactus of concealment, bound to be one soon."*

"How about behind that billboard?" Hassler asks.

"Looks good to me," Kesey says. *"Someone poke Kathy and see if she wants to stretch her legs. She's been crashed since we left Wikieup."*

"She's up," Hagen says. *"No poking needed."*

The bus pulls over to the side.

"OK. Men to the right, women to the left," Hassler says. *"Go to the other side of the billboard, Kathy. The other side."*

Wearing only a bra and panties, Kathy dives headfirst into a clump of flowers.

"No, Kathy!" Hassler yells. *"Not in there. Don't roll around in there. Oh great Mary mother of Jesus and all his sibling rivals!"*

"Such beauty . . . just like a little baby," she cries, rolling in the clump. Then she begins to scream.

PRANKSTER MIKE HAGEN'S CHECK FOR $3.00, MADE OUT TO NEAL CASSADY, WHO USED IT TO BUY GASOLINE. (RON BEVIRT)

"S.O.S., S.O.S!" Hassler yells. "Give me a hand. Help me pull her out."

Babbs reaches for her.

"Son of a bitch!" Babbs exclaims. "They're stickier'n nails and twice as sharp. Yeek!"

"Get out of the way, Babbs," Kesey says. "Let me in there. I've got shoes on."

"Yow! Wish I did. What are those things anyway?"

"Goatheads. Three-pronged stickers hiding on the stems underneath the flowers. Poor Kathy. She's covered with them."

He and Hassler lift her up.

"Take it off!" Kathy screams. "They're underneath the strap. Take it off!"

Kesey quickly obliges.

"Hey, you did that like a pro," Hassler says. "One-handed too."

"Years of back seat experience. Look at that. The goathead lumps are turning purple. They match her areolas."

"Oh for Christ's sake, Kesey," Jane says. "You're disgusting. But what would you expect from a man? Here, Kathy, let me help you."

She puts a blanket around Kathy's bare shoulders.

"Yeah, get her aboard before we get busted for indecent exposure," Babbs says. "And someone find the tweezers. I've got a thousand stickers in my feet."

"Boar-oard!" Cassady yells. "All aboard for Houston. Next stop, Houston."

Chapter 4—Houston

Houston. Rice University. Quenby Street. Shading oaks. Birds chirruping. Manicured lawns. Respectable homes. A curtain pulls back from a front window and a bespectacled eye peers out.

"See anything yet?" a female voice calls from the kitchen.

"They called from Flatonia, so it should be a few minutes yet," Larry McMurtry says.

Novelist, writer of Horseman, Pass By (made into the movie Hud), Larry was a classmate of Kesey's at Stanford's graduate writing program four years earlier. He stands poised, his son in his arms. "Oh, God!" he says, dropping the curtain.

"What is it, dear?" his wife calls.

LARRY MCMURTRY, NOVELIST AND KESEY'S STANFORD CLASSMATE, WITH HIS SON JAMES, DURING A PRANKSTER STOPOVER AT HIS HOUSE IN HOUSTON. (RON BEVIRT)

"It's them. But what a them."

"What do you mean?"

"It's indescribable. You'll have to see for yourself."

Shifting the boy into his other arm, he goes outside. A shrill laugh comes from the bus. Larry walks to the curb and the bus door opens.

"Oh, Frankie, Frankie!" Kathy shrieks, stepping out of the bus and out of her blanket. She tugs at Larry's son.

"Ma'am," Larry says in a soft drawl. "Ma'am, would you please let go? The boy is crying, ma'am. . . ."

Cassady pops out with the blanket.

"We all have children back home, m'dear, and even our hardened hearts are suffused with longing; but you must admit, this is not the one. . . ."

"Wow!" John says, head out the window. *"What a shot! Did you get it Hassler?"*

Hassler turns, 35-millimeter camera in hand. *"I was ready, but the shock was too much. I forgot to click the shutter. Did you see that? She was naked. Stark naked!"*

Kesey steps off the bus and he and Larry shake hands. Larry's wife comes out and there are introductions all around.

"Make yourselves at home," Larry tells everyone, and the Pranksters troop inside, escorting Kathy. Larry looks at them nervously.

"She going to be all right?" he asks Kesey.

"I hope so. Strung out is all. If she can make it through the next day or so it ought to wear off."

"Better keep an eye on her. I just hope no one witnessed that exhibition outside. They're pretty straight folks around here, you know."

"Hey!" Babbs says. *"Straight is as straight does. Like an arrow, varoom! Not to worry, we got it under control."*

"Hummmm," Larry murmurs, looking over the top of his glasses.

Chapter 5—She's Gone!

Nighttime in Houston. Cicadas cackling in the trees. Snores answering on the back lawn and from inside the house. A dark shape rises and goes out the open door and down the sidewalk. A dog barks. Clouds cover the moon. A thin band of light appears in the eastern sky.

"Hey, wake up!" Hassler shouts. *"Wake up, you guys. She's gone."*

"Oh, no," Jane says. *"Nice going, Dale. You were supposed to be on watch."*

"Hey! She was sound asleep. I was right next to her. No way she could have gotten up without me hearing her."

"Well, she's gone now. Someone go wake up Kesey and Babbs."

Chapter 6—Search Party

"Full speed ahead," Kesey says, leading the way to Larry's car. *"Guess we better cruise the neighborhood first."*

"Yes, at eyes that peer at eyes peering back at bushes and lawns behind oaks and maples smelling of magnolia blossoms draped across supine forms," Babbs says. *"But nary a one promising glimpses of stark-naked limbs and long-flowing tresses."*

"This is about the extent of the houses. From here on in it gets into the business area and I don't think she'd be out there in the open very long before she got picked up," Larry says.

"Better return to home port," Kesey says, *"see if there's been any report."*

"Has there ever!" Hagen yells when the car pulls up. *"We got a call from her boyfriend in San Francisco. His name is Hankin. He's on The Committee, that humor theater group? She phoned him from jail. The cops picked her up. Now it's happening. Hankin is arriving Houston 403 United 6:11 for pickup and delivery, gives us just enough time to meet him at the gate."*

"Board!" Cassady yells, hitting the starter on the bus. *"Bo-oard!"*

NEAL CASSADY AND KATHY CASANO—"STARK NAKED"—ON THE BEACH IN WIKIEUP, ARIZONA. (RON BEVIRT)

THE BUS ON ITS CROSS-COUNTRY TRIP. KEN BABBS EXPLAINS WHY THE BUS WAS PAINTED: "AMERICA REALLY REPRESENTS FREEDOM. . . .
[AND WE WERE CONCERNED WITH] TAKING PAINTING BACK FROM THE PAINTERS. ALSO, THIS BUS NEEDED SOME BRIGHT COLORS."
(RON BEVIRT)

Chapter 7—Reconnaissance

"Navigator's report!" Kesey yells from on top.

"Parkway dead ahead," John says. "Follow signs straight to airport. Notice the airplane on the sign, angling in for a landing."

"Instrument corrections not needed," Cassady says. "Second gear permission denied. Yellow light. Red second automatic! Automatic second, sir. Oh, we gotta go left and we're in the right lane! Request turn, sir."

"Are we clear to the rear, dear?" Babbs asks.

"Liquid, we got to have liquid," Kesey says.

"Right after this station wagon," Hagen says.

"Go cars, go!" Cassady shouts. "Easing forward."

"Clear! All clear!" Hagen shouts.

"Liquid to the top. Airport dead ahead," Babbs says. "What's the recognition signal?"

"Blue shirt. Black pants. Slicked back hair and a Roman patrician nose. All bedecking a serious, six-foot frame looking wildly around for a plain, nondescript bus."

"Target in sight," Kesey calls from the top. "And now he's spotted us and is cringing. Don't let him escape. Target crouching behind baggage cart," Kesey says. "Activate outdoor speakers. HANKIN! WE HAVE SPOTTED YOU. DO NOT RESIST. THESE PEOPLE ARE HERE TO HELP YOU. WELCOME ABOARD."

"This way, please," Babbs says, escorting Hankin to the ladder that goes up through the turret.

Chapter 8—Forge Ahead

"Hello," Hankin tells the police. "We're looking for a lost person. Is she there? She's about five feet six inches, black hair, shoulder-length. She's wearing a black skirt, no shoes, no identification; I don't think she has a purse, even. Kathy Casano. It's Spanish origin. She's 25. She has one child. Me? I'm Larry Hankin. What are you going to do with my name? OK, information only. I'm from San Francisco and so is she. She came to Houston on a job. To make a movie here and took about a week of travelling to get here. I stayed in San Francisco. What it boils down to is I should never have let her go alone. I got a call from her yesterday and she sounded like she was in trouble and I took a plane here and when I got here she had disappeared. The people who live here say they saw her about three in the morning.

"How long have I known her? Six months. I'm really worried about her. What? Childhood diseases? I don't know. She had her baby in the hospital. Why? Is she blacked out? No. Thank God. Where is the police station? Capital Avenue? Fourth floor. OK. Thank you very much, sir."

He puts the phone down.

"God, it's the homicide department," Hagen says, starting the bus. "It's my fault, too. All my fault. She was perfectly straight before all this. And then she flipped out."

"You got to be very cool with that stuff," Hankin tells Hagen. *"It's not your fault. Kesey's in charge of this fucking mess. I don't blame him either, though. She's got a great face. Great for photographing."*

"I just didn't know," Hagen says. *"I was sitting outside last night and I knew where she was and I thought she was all right and suddenly she was gone."*

"When somebody's in trouble, you help them," Hankin says. *"Film that. But to just let somebody go . . . to see them crack up . . . she told me she was kidnapped . . . I didn't sense it . . . she made a joke of it . . . said perhaps her condescending airs would turn them off . . . like when she was starting acting classes at the university."*

They pull up to the police station.

"Well," Kesey says, back at Larry's house, *"guess we better be shovelling along, as Digby O'Dell the friendly undertaker used to say. Sorry we can't partake of this Texan horse-pitality any longer but the rigors of the schedule and all. Gotta be in New York City, you know —"* Extending the hand, clasping and shaking, and it's into the bus they go and away with a roar, saying good-byes from the roof, out the windows, full of relief and heartache, fretting and laughing, roaring out of town with the speakers on full, top-to-bottom communication intact, Cassady at the wheel, Hagen with his eye to the Arriflex and the whole feelthy affair of the bleeped-out lady seemingly forgotten except —

— except Babbs yells, *"Pull over! Pull over!"* and in the confusion of the unexplained stop, he vaults from the bus door and across the sidewalk and into a small office, to emerge ten minutes later waving a piece of paper and saying, *"I did it, we are now free of all moral outrage and guilt trips baying at our behinds."*

"What is that fool talking about now?" Jane asks.

"Well, it was the Western Union office, so it must be about a telegram," Dale says. *"But to whom and concerning what?"*

"What else but a note of succor to our dearly departed fellow traveller?" Babbs says, reading a scrap of paper. *"TO KATHY AKA STARK NAKED CARE OF HOUSTON POLICE DEPARTMENT FOURTH FLOOR. CONGRATS ON FINE PERFORMANCE STOP CAPTURED ON FILM AND TAPE STOP FUTURE STARDOM ASSURED STOP PRESSING DEMANDS OF SHOOTING SCHEDULE FORCES DEPARTURE STOP CONTINUED SUCCESS AND WELL WISHES FROM THE MERRY BAND END."*

— "The Intrepid Traveller"

R.O. to L.I
R.I. " R.F.
L.I " L.F.
" O, " "
R.F. " L.O.
L.F. " L.I
R.I. to R / L.O.
to / R (over)

R.O. to L.I.
R.I " L.F.
L. " " R.O.
" O. " L. "
R.F. + L.F.
OPtioNAL
9nside R's.

From Houston, the Pranksters ploughed through the deep, hot South, tripping and filming. They stopped in New Orleans, their unabashed carnival exuberance attracting interest from the locals and questions from the police. Then they made an abortive visit to a segregated beach in Lake Pontchartrain, Louisiana, where they drew a curious crowd with the amplified recorded music blasting from the bus. The crowd encircled the bus, the police advised the tripping Pranksters to leave, and they did.

FIRST COP STOP OF THE BUS TRIP. KEN BABBS REMEMBERS THE OFFICER SAYING: "NOW, DON'T TELL ME THE BRAKE LIGHTS ON THE MOTORCYCLE ARE SUPPOSED TO SERVE FOR THE WHOLE DARN BUS—WE'RE NOT *THAT* LOOSE, JUST BECAUSE YOU'VE GOT CALIFORNIA PLATES." (RON BEVIRT)

DRIVER NEAL CASSADY'S ROTATION CHART FOR THE TIRES ON THE PRANKSTERS' BUS. (RON BEVIRT)

"INTO NEW ORLEANS"

*T*he Pranksters stopped in New Orleans at a place called "The Absinthe Bar." Inside, a hunched-over guy wearing a fedora slunk over his eyes slouches over the piano, banging out a three-bar blues.

I've been from town to town, seems to me it was always the same . . . *the guy sings, big oily puddles of Prankster eyes staring up at him. He's the most beautiful thing they've ever seen. The best piano player, the best singer . . .* Some folks call me bad news . . .

They haul the movie cameras and tape recorders, and begin turning this man into a star. They dub him Moonlight Sinatra. And at the base of Canal Street, in the dust motes and the sunny air, Moonlight Sinatra thinks at first that the Pranksters are putting him on, then he realizes, hey, they're telling me the truth, they do like me! His voice gets prettier and his piano playing gets better. The people in the other room stop laughing and listen. He knows he'll never find a better audience in the whole world than this. He decides he'll join up on this bus and he goes out and gets on the bus and everyone notices he's got a game leg, a twisted little leg, and, when he sits down on the bus after being up for three straight days and after having a fight with his dad in the welding shop, he opens his legs and a wave of funk is released that's like to knock the Pranksters right out of the bus.

"Whoa," Cassady says, "let's move a little bit farther down the line!"

Moonlight Sinatra doesn't even last the ride to Lake Pontchartrain. He falls sound asleep and doesn't budge until James Brown and the Famous Flames rouse him from his stupor.

The Pranksters are floating in inner tubes, playing their instruments. They love music, it's in the Beat tradition, and they love jazz in particular—because of the free form, the coming on in a nonverbal but very emotional way. They express the feelings, little knowing, in their pranking, bass-ackward way, they are integrating Lake Pontchartrain. They're swimming in the "Colored Only" section.

The kids bring sticks out in the water and begin to slap the water with their sticks, beating out a rhythm accompaniment.

"We're here in the River Styx," Zonk yells.

"And we better get the Hades out," Babbs yells back.

He's picked up on some sort of uncomfortable feeling. They've intruded on turf not of their own making, and so they split, much to the disappointment of the stick-beating rhythm devils left scratching their heads and wondering what those people were all about.

"Man, you see them cats floating on inner tubes playing them horns?" one local fella asks.

"Yeah, but didn't sound like no music to me!" his buddy responds.

"What'd that one big tall cat say, 'Form of nonverbal communication'. . . . "

"Yeah, but with what?"

"There's that egret," Moonlight Sinatra mumbles. The blue New Orleans egret flies across the hood as they're trying to leave. A bull snake is in the road. Dale plays his violin. Whenever they run across bull snakes it always excites Dale like that. All he has to do is see one bull snake on the road and he begins playing the violin every time.

NEAL CASSADY: "YOU HAVE TO USE THE SAME BODY YOU BEGIN THE SYMPHONY WITH, Y'SEE? BUT THAT'S THE THING—GROUP EXPERIENCE. WHAT IS THERE BUT ONE FORCE? THAT IS, OF THE SOUL?" (RON BEVIRT)

They never see Moonlight Sinatra again after Lake Pontchartrain. It was either join up with the bus or go back to the welding shop. He opts for the welding shop. They drop him off at the Greyhound station.

Man cleaning up behind them says, "That bus came through here left the biggest mess they've ever seen on those docks. The cops are hunting for that bus, and know it's someplace in New Orleans. Firemen are hosing down the streets after it's been by."

Kesey leans against a patrol car door, eating a watermelon while talking to the lawman. The cop's shiny-bright sunglasses reflect the black watermelon seeds Kesey spits, arcing toward the ground.

"We can be trusted to drive an enormous bus all the way around the nation," Kesey tells him, "but not a Mustang around the Bay Area. It doesn't matter how much security and credit and community good will and social prestige that you build up, all you have to do is push the right button and it's blown. That's our great talent. We're unerring in searching out those buttons."

"I don't know any thang 'bout that," the cop says, "but if'n I was you I'd push the button that starts that bus and takes you all the hell out of my county."

— "The Intrepid Traveller"

(RIGHT) KEN BABBS RELAXING IN TEXAS: "ONCE YOU LEARN WHAT A PRANK IS AND HOW A PRANK WORKS, YOU GOT TO FOLLOW THE RULES AND YOU CAN'T GO HURT ANYBODY, AND AFTER IT'S OVER, EVERYBODY LAUGHS AND FEELS GOOD ABOUT IT. YOU'RE NOT PUTTING SOMETHING DOWN OR TURNING SOMEONE INTO AN ENEMY." (LEFT) GEORGE LAMBRECHT — "ZONKER" — PLAYING MANDOLIN IN A SWIMMING POOL IN TEXAS. (RON BEVIRT)

The next stops for the bus were in towns in Mississippi and Alabama that were connected by U.S. Route 90. On they went: into Florida, stopping in Pensacola before continuing up north into Georgia; through the Blue Ridge Mountains; and finally, New York City.

In Manhattan they had the use of an apartment on the Upper East Side, thanks to California friend Chloe Scott, who was in town housesitting for her aunt. It was here that the Pranksters staged the party that brought Kesey, Cassady, and the Pranksters together with Allen Ginsberg, Peter Orlovsky, and Jack Kerouac.

ALLEN GINSBERG: Neal drove out to Northport without any notice, to where Jack was living with his mother. Kerouac had liked Kesey's book and thought that Kesey was a regular, real writer and granted him that status.

But he himself was reticent to come into the city because whenever he did he drank too much and got ill. So, he was a little grumpy about being taken out, but he went anyway.

ROBERT STONE: My wife and I were already back East when the bus trip started. But when the Pranksters got back there, some of them came and lived with us in our West Side apartment and others just kept living on the bus.

The night of the party they came and got me, and we drove in the bus across Central Park to the apartment that Chloe Scott had lined up.

ALLEN GINSBERG: I think it was ten or eleven at night when Neal brought Jack to the apartment on Park Avenue where Kesey was staying. Neal and Jack stayed down in the bus with Peter Orlovsky and myself for a while, while I tried to take a picture of the bus in the dark. Then we went upstairs.

"PASSING THE TORCH"

World War II laid a bloody pall over the land. Mercy and goodness were swallowed by cannons and bombs. The Beats and Beboppers kept the spark alive. Freedom rose out of the ashes in Parker's sax, Kerouac's books, Ginsberg's poetry, in Cassady's raps. Cassady roared into the apartment and told them the news: "I've found Ginsberg and he's bringing Orlovsky. I'm driving out to Long Island to get Kerouac."

The news that Ginsberg, Orlovsky, and Kerouac are coming to the apartment galvanizes the Pranksters into action. Clothes are swooped off the chairs and stashed behind the doors. Fresh film is inserted in the cameras. Blank tape in the recorders. Instruments up and ready: the two-flute, stand-up bass, sax, clarinet, drums. Fingers nervously tapping, coffee perking, drinks poured; all is ready.

They don't count on the surprise guest: Julius, Peter Orlovsky's brother. Having been in a state hospital, it's his first night out and he is in hawg heaven. The wonderful bus. The wonderful people. The lickety-split talk. And Cassady whisking from person to person, the ecstatic host: "Dig this, Jack, the tape recorders and the cameras, just like we used to do, only this time professionally!"

Jack is unimpressed. He wasn't too interested in this event, but it would be good to see Neal again, and he reluctantly agreed to come and now he sits glumly on the sofa while Ginsberg leads everyone in a Hari-Hie-Hee-Jingle-Jangle-Tinklee-Bells-Krishna chant.

"Take a listen," Cassady says, putting the earphones on Jack. The Pranksters massage Kerouac with soothing words. They croon choruses of "Everything's Fine," into his ears. Dale covers Jack's shoulders with an American flag. Jack endures it stoically and when the chorusing is done, takes off the earphones and carefully folds the flag and places it on the sofa.

A little while later, he leaves. "Seemed tired," Babbs says. But before a long-winded discussion of the case can begin, someone reports that Julius is missing. The search locates him on the bus. He wants to live there. Sadly, he cannot, and Peter must take him home.

The party has come to an end. Everyone is still jacked up. What was the import?

POET PETER ORLOVSKY AND BROTHER JULIUS AT THE MANHATTAN PARTY. (RON BEVIRT)

Did we click? It isn't until much later that it becomes clear: The Psychedelic Revolution was flooding the whole universe, not just a few acid minds, a medium through which the wavelength travels. The torch had been passed from the Beat to the Psychedelic, with Cassady as the driver, the tour guide, the swing man, foot in both eras, the flame passing from Kerouac to Kesey.

—"The Intrepid Traveller"

KEN KESEY (LEFT) AND JACK
KEROUAC (RIGHT) AT THE
MANHATTAN PARTY. POET ALLEN
GINSBERG ON THE MEETING
BETWEEN KEROUAC AND THE
PRANKSTERS: "[THE PRANKSTERS]
WERE YOUNG, EAGER, OVER-
NOISY, NOT PAYING ATTENTION
TO HIM PROPERLY AND TRYING TO
SHOW HIM THEIR ACT, RATHER
THAN RESPECTING HIM AS AN
ELDER AND BEING QUIET AND
LISTENING AND TREATING HIM
MORE GENTLY. THEY WANTED HIM
TO JOIN THEIR BIG PARTY."
(RON BEVIRT)

ROBERT STONE: Of course Kerouac was very drunk. He was drinking whiskey from a paper bag and he was very pissed-off and at his most embittered.

ALLEN GINSBERG: The Pranksters had a big throne of a sofa completely clear for Kerouac. The room was full of wires and lights and cameras and people in striped clothes and Pranksters and jesters and American flags and people waving cameras around drinking in rock and roll and all lit up like amphetamines.

Kerouac came in. He was mute and quiet and they showed him to his couch seat but there was an American flag on it, so Kerouac, without making a big, noisy complaint but a little minor objection, turned around and took the flag and folded it up neatly and put it over the side of the couch so they wouldn't sit on it. He was very conscious of the flag as an image, and I think he misunderstood their use of it. They were appropriating the flag for their own Americana purposes and he thought they were maybe insulting it. Of course, you can say many things about Kesey, but being unpatriotic isn't one of them.

ROBERT STONE: Kerouac was a guy who was basically very sweet who soured over the years. I think alcohol and the ridicule from the press were really getting to him. His nature was becoming embittered. He was becoming very hostile.

What did he have to be embittered about? Well, instead of treating Kerouac as a serious author, he was treated as a joke. He encouraged it in a way because he was always showing up drunk and clowning, but the columnists, the newspapers, and the magazines really did treat Kerouac like a joke. There was that terrible thing that Truman Capote said about his work: "This isn't writing, this is typing."

In those days there was this nasty hostility toward nonconformists, and Kerouac endured a lot of it.

ALLEN GINSBERG: Anyway, Kerouac didn't say much and was quite ill. He was also ill at ease, not because of Kesey but because of his physical condition. The Pranksters misunderstood it and thought that he was not with them, or rejecting them. But Kesey was smart enough to recognize Kerouac and respect him for what he was doing. And right then, by the way, Kerouac had just finished writing one of his great novels, *Vanity of Duluoz.*

ROBERT STONE: It was funny though that Kerouac couldn't find solace in people like Ginsberg, Orlovsky, Corso, and even us. I think you have to put a lot of it simply down to alcohol. I think that really ruined him.

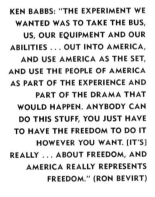

KEN BABBS: "THE EXPERIMENT WE WANTED WAS TO TAKE THE BUS, US, OUR EQUIPMENT AND OUR ABILITIES . . . OUT INTO AMERICA, AND USE AMERICA AS THE SET, AND USE THE PEOPLE OF AMERICA AS PART OF THE EXPERIENCE AND PART OF THE DRAMA THAT WOULD HAPPEN. ANYBODY CAN DO THIS STUFF, YOU JUST HAVE TO HAVE THE FREEDOM TO DO IT HOWEVER YOU WANT. [IT'S] REALLY . . . ABOUT FREEDOM, AND AMERICA REALLY REPRESENTS FREEDOM." (RON BEVIRT)

Still, I was surprised at his embitteredness. My wife was a waitress in an espresso coffee house before we went West so I had seen him around giving readings. So I was certainly surprised. We were certainly in awe of him, but he was very nasty to all of us.

ALLEN GINSBERG: As for the other Pranksters, I don't know what they thought of Kerouac and I don't know how much of his writing they had read except *On the Road*. I don't even know if the company there knew the depth of his achievement. I don't think Kesey did fully either until the eighties, when he actually sat down and read through a lot of Kerouac's work besides *On the Road*. But, for that one book, Kesey did see him as sort of an elder master and a great American.

STEVE LAMBRECHT: I didn't know who Kerouac was. I remember someone pointing him out in the apartment as being a famous person. He didn't have a lot to say and he was drunk on top of it.

ALLEN GINSBERG: The rest of the Pranksters wanted him to join their big party. But Kerouac was in no condition to join anyone's party. He

ALLEN GINSBERG: "KEROUAC DIDN'T SAY MUCH, AND WAS QUITE ILL. HE WAS ALSO ILL AT EASE, NOT BECAUSE OF KESEY BUT BECAUSE OF HIS PHYSICAL CONDITION. [THE PRANKSTERS] MISUNDERSTOOD IT AND THOUGHT THAT HE WAS NOT WITH THEM, OR REJECTING THEM. BUT KESEY WAS SMART ENOUGH TO RECOGNIZE KEROUAC AND RESPECT HIM FOR WHAT HE WAS DOING." (RON BEVIRT)

was an alcoholic and had been for five or six years, and was suffering from it, and hesitated to go into the city at all, much less go into the city for a big party full of people who were drowning in LSD five years after he'd had psychedelics and fourteen years after his first peyote. Of course they didn't realize the nature of his condition because they weren't paying attention.

ROBERT STONE: I think Kerouac was a little jealous and angry at Neal. Here Neal had fallen in with what looked to him like Stanford fraternity types. We were a lot younger than he was and everybody was tremendously healthy. I think he felt that we were just a bunch of California kids. As a result, he was very nasty.

ALLEN GINSBERG: This was also a bit of a reunion for Kerouac and Neal, who hadn't been together since 1959. But Neal was taking a lot of amphetamines and acid at the time of this party, so he was not really warm, consoling company. He was more nervous and frantic.

He did put himself out trying to accommodate Kerouac, but, in a way, that was nerve-wracking because he had roused Kerouac without any notice, and driven him back to the city to a big party full of people who were taking amphetamines and acid and running around with cameras and klieg lights in the middle of an apartment on Park Avenue where they might be raided by police for smoking grass.

STEVE LAMBRECHT: That night Peter Orlovsky's brother Julius shit in his shoe inside of the bus. We were driving around town when someone yelled, "Jesus Christ, he shit in his shoe! What did you shit in your shoe for, Julius?" Julius was trying to make sense of it by saying that he needed to take a shit and he felt as though if he did it in his shoe he could get rid of it easier.

KEN BABBS: Before the bus trip we were talking about "rapping" novels out instead of typing—because typing is so slow. We were going to take acid and stay up all night and rap out novels and tape record them. Then, to add things, we were going to act out parts, and then do the music that went with it, and then, finally, we started talking about getting the

KEN KESEY PLAYS THE FLUTE AT
THE MANHATTAN PARTY. KESEY
LATER SAID: "NONE OF US ARE
MUSICIANS OR NAVIGATORS OR
TECHNICIANS. WE'RE ALL
COMPLETELY BUMBLING
AMATEURS . . . LIKE GALILEO OR
COLUMBUS OR ANYBODY WHO
MAKES ANY SORT OF DISCOVERY
AT ALL IN THIS WORLD, THEY
HAVE TO DO IT BY ACCIDENT."
(RON BEVIRT)

movie cameras and filming it. So we were very swiftly going from a novel on a page to novels on audio-tape to novels on film.

The thing that Cassady gave us was his ability to come on in a meaningful way, extemporizing. He was just doing his thing off the cuff. He worked at it constantly and by the time we got to Manhattan he was going full bore, his chops really down.

The night of the big apartment party, after the evening's luminaries had departed, Neal was still holding forth.

"A CASSADY RAP"

"*You know, for those of us who had the background like I did,*" Hassler says, "*conservative, middle-class scene,* On the Road *was the most tremendous trip for us because we found out all about this gassy, groovy stuff going on. It was the first word that we got. This is why* Howl *is our holy thing. The basic sheer scream that tore along our backs—the first thing that opened us up, that let us dig these messages coming from what you guys were bringing in. You know, it would really be a gas if we could get somebody to set up a foundation where people could go who were really trying to increase their psychic powers.*"

"*Yes,*" Cassady says, "*to channel these sensitivities you're talking about. There's one village in Holland where the whole place is a nut house. They don't talk or anything. They can't talk. The whole village is attuned! That's where you'd go. . . . It's all very well, taking twelve hits a day, but what's the health? It's the same problem as with India. Self. In other words, over there, all those fakirs are holding their arse for a thousand years, or standing on their nose for self! It's a hang-up. We're not here for self; we're here for service. We're here to multiply. Subdue ye the earth and all that. We're here to make like three-dimensional chess. We're here to accentuate. In other words . . . we're made in the image of co-creator, companion, and we want to be outgoing. It pleases us. What is left? Giving. . . .*"

"Salty dog, salty dog, don't want to be your man at all. Honey, let me be your salty dog. I knew you were a nonce from the look of your worn-out shoes. Let me be your salty dog. *She put my car in second gear. It had two ranges, like a Pontiac, high, and the low and middle ranges together. Wide open at 85 and she said, 'I thought that motor was awful loud,' when at Burlingame fifty miles later right through the block—BLANG!-goes the rod! Oh, I see we are ready to go. . . . Bo-ard! Board!*"

—"The Intrepid Traveller"

NEAL CASSADY AT THE WHEEL ON THE ROAD TO MILLBROOK. (ALLEN GINSBERG)

And so, at the suggestion of Allen Ginsberg, the bus left the party in Manhattan to go to Millbrook, New York, to pay a visit to Timothy Leary and his Castalia Foundation, where a group led by Ralph Metzner, Richard Alpert, and others was conducting ongoing experiments with LSD.

RON BEVIRT: William Hitchcock had gotten involved at Harvard with Leary and Alpert, and gave them this place to live. They needed a nice quiet scene to explore inner space and had been there for maybe a year or so.

They were doing a lot of academic research. I mean, they weren't just taking acid and riding the subway. They were setting up in a room with a group of people who would take acid, and they would have candles burning and incense and stuff.

The model that [the Pranksters] were all embarked on was more of one that had us getting high and falling out on the streets and seeing what happened.

RAM DASS: There was no forewarning whatsoever that the Pranksters were going to show up at Millbrook. Our situation was as follows: The night before there were about twenty of us. We had all done acid and it turned out to be a very intense and profound trip. We sat by the fire, all of us huddled together. There was a lot of intimacy and profundity and it was a very deep trip that had gone on all night long. By seven or eight in the morning, everybody was in mellow, delicate, vulnerable space and drifting off to bed for the day. It was at this very moment that the bus drove up.

It was perfect timing as usual. They had energy that was so disparate from what was going on at the house. They were very speedy. We were mellowing out.

They were so preoccupied with their own agenda that I didn't feel that they really heard us at all. Nonetheless, I went out and welcomed them.

RON BEVIRT: So we rolled in there, and set off a green smoke grenade that blew green smoke right through the open windows into their house. And their house was kind of enveloped in green smoke. It was like the Huns coming to visit Camelot.

"I F I F"

"You gotta make it up to Timothy Leary's IFIF scene up in Millbrook while you're here," Ginsberg says.

"IFIF, what's that?" Kesey asks.

"International Federation for Internal Freedom," Ginsberg says. "The whole Hitchcock fortune's behind it, and they've turned the family mansion into a scientific center to have researchers experiment on themselves with LSD."

"Great," Kesey says, "Is-is comes to if-if".

"ISIS, what's that?" Ginsberg asks.

"Intrepid Search for Inner Space."

Cassady swings the bus in toward the gate. A stone two-story tower is alongside. Kesey goes topside to report the clearance conditions. He wades through feathers; kicks them overboard. Shrill trumpet notes from the upper registers and a bearded face pops out of a turret window.

"Who goeth and what foreth and why trail ye these feathereth?"

"We be the Merry Band in search of the Inner Freedomites," Kesey responds. "We have gone through a vivid chick storm, no need to lithp.

"Okay," Kesey says. "We're coming in. Intrepid Traveller?"

"Yes, Sir Swash."

"We're about to make a landing at the ancestral mansion of the Merry Band of Pranksters. It is certainly a bright arrival."

"Smoke bomb delight," Cassady says.

"Keep moving forward," Kesey says. "That way we can leave the smoke behind—emerge from it like a battleship out of the fog."

The bomb's green smoke billows from in front of the bus. Out of the smoke toots and tweets of whistles and flutes announce their arrival: the bus turning onto a paved road in front of the portico; behind it the towering stone mansion with louvered windows and towering chimneys; double doors opening, and bikinied slim women carrying children and garlands and bowls of steaming rice; behind them a bespectacled smiling balding man dressed in chinos and a Hawaiian shirt.

"Ah, look at the lovely ladies," Cassady says. *"We'll do this scene in three reverse movements."*

They emerge from the green smoke pulling to a stop in the turnaround in front of the mansion, greeted by Richard Alpert and the lovely lithe bikinied maidens; Pranksters tootling and fluting the arrival; Babbs and Cassady and Kesey and Ginsberg leading the handshaking charge, followed closely behind by the rest of the Merry Band.

PRANKSTER PHOTOGRAPHER RON BEVIRT RESTING IN THE BUS IN MILLBROOK, AS OTHER PRANKSTERS SETTLE DOWN FOR AN AFTERNOON NAP AFTER THE DRIVE UP FROM NEW YORK CITY. SANDY LEHMANN-HAUPT IS VISIBLE FILMING THROUGH THE BACK WINDOW. (ALLEN GINSBERG)

TIM LEARY VISITING CASSADY ON THE BUS, WHICH IS PARKED IN THE DRIVEWAY OF THE MILLBROOK HOUSE. (ALLEN GINSBERG)

"You all look pretty exhausted and strung out," says Richard Alpert, Leary's colleague. "Well, unwind and cool down in our waterfall. You can wash off some of those feathers."

The Pranksters strip down to their undies and gambol in the frolicky waters, but not quietly—hooting and carousing like a bunch of western wild flowers.

"I feel like we're a pastoral Indian village invaded by a whooping cowboy band of Wild West saloon carousers," Alpert says to the lithe young ladies.

—"The Intrepid Traveller"

RAM DASS: They came in with the idea that this was going to be a meeting between East and West, the acid tribes of the different coasts. I don't think our group was into any part of the myth. They expected a sort of summit meeting, kind of a swim, dope, food, hanging out, talking, Tim Leary and Kesey, and all those people. A session where everyone was wise about the universe.

The problem was they came in on the tail end of our acid trip. They ended up feeling kind of rejected and I don't think very warmly welcomed.

Still, they were allowed to roam around the Millbrook mansion, which was a 63-room, baronial, Italian stone palace owned by Hitchcock.

TIMOTHY LEARY: I had just fallen in love with a woman who later became my wife, so, needless to say, that was number one on my consciousness. Not only was I lovesick, but I had also come down with a heavy flu. So I went right to my room and went to bed. Put yourself in my place. I didn't know this was history being made, a meeting of the acid tribes. I was preoccupied with other things.

RAM DASS: In many ways it was a moment in history that didn't happen. Leary retired to his room and didn't come forth. I think that he really didn't have an identity with those people at that time. Later, when he got busted, he started to make a street identity.

TIMOTHY LEARY: We had positive feelings toward Kesey's group, but we were aware that they were different. We used words like "session" and we talked about "lysergic acid" and they were talking about "tripping out on acid." The language of the psychedelic culture came from the streets and dance halls and the buses. They were making fun of us for being so formal.

RAM DASS: There were great philosophical differences between us and the Pranksters, even though both groups were searching for something. I think that the Pranksters, at that time, were making more of a social-political statement than we were. Millbrook was primarily a research-oriented space that was trying to understand human consciousness.

ON THE PORCH OF THE CASTALIA
FOUNDATION HOUSE IN
MILLBROOK, N.Y. LEFT TO RIGHT:
RON BEVIRT (SEATED WITH BACK TO
CAMERA), UNIDENTIFIED MAN,
SUSAN METZNER, KEN BABBS (WITH
STICK), KEN KESEY, GEORGE
WALKER, AND SANDY LEHMANN-
HAUPT. ALLEN GINSBERG: "TOO
MANY BUS PEOPLE TO COME INSIDE
THE BIG CASTALIA FOUNDATION
HOUSE; THEY SETTLED HERE
OUTDOORS TO FIGURE OUT THE
OCCASION." (ALLEN GINSBERG)

We were doing things like setting up the experimental typewriter. It was a keyboard that had different states of emotion and planes of consciousness on it instead of letters. Since you couldn't speak in all of these states you could keep some record of what you were going through as you passed through it.

We took turns guiding each other through sessions, so that one of us would use the *Tao*, and one of us would use the *I Ching*, so we could create various settings.

I did slide shows for people who were alcoholics or who were having marriage breakdowns. We were seeing what kind of therapeutic value acid had.

It is too perjorative to say that we were elitists, but I think that we definitely were playing it differently than the Pranksters.

TIMOTHY LEARY: I wouldn't say that our experiments at Millbrook were exactly scientific. We were keeping records, and trying to develop maps and guidebooks of the mind. We were exploring the brain. We were not just dosing people to see what would happen. Our motto was that we would offer the experience with one or more of us taking, sharing the experience and then coming back like neuro-nauts to tell about what we saw.

Though influenced by clinical methods, this research was, in effect, an eclectic, constantly changing social experiment intended to unearth various paths to enlightenment.

TIMOTHY LEARY: You know, Millbrook went on for five years. During that time, a lot of people came and would spend a day or a week and then leave. That place changed every 72 hours. You'd be there one weekend and we would be doing tai chi and the next weekend we would be following Allistair Crowley. It was changing all the time, depending upon the moods.

BABA RAM DASS: I remember them staying around for the day. I remember sitting on the porch railing talking to them. We all went out to the little tennis house where people would go for a week of silent retreat and they did sort of a ceremony out there. Then they took a bath and ate and slept. They really did little more than that.

It was fairly disappointing for them. They caught us about twelve

DR. RICHARD ALPERT (LATER KNOWN AS RAM DASS) ON THE PORCH AT THE IFIF MANSION IN MILLBROOK: "IF [THE PRANKSTERS] HAD COME THE NIGHT BEFORE IT WOULD HAVE BEEN AN ENTIRELY DIFFERENT STORY FOR ALL OF US FOR THE REST OF OUR LIVES. BUT THAT'S THE WAY IT IS. I LIVE IN A WORLD WHERE THERE IS NO ERROR, SO THAT IS WHAT WAS MEANT TO HAPPEN." (RON BEVIRT)

hours too late; it was nothing more than that. If they had come the night before, it would have been an entirely different story for all of us for the rest of our lives. But that's the way it is. I live in a world where there is no error, so that is what was meant to happen.

TIMOTHY LEARY: I'm not sure what the real intention of them coming to Millbrook was anyway, except just to say "hi." It is the nature of the tribe that they don't meld. The genius of the tribal system is that each one has its own totem and its own gods. When you get into merging tribes you get into feudalism. The very nature of the stuff is that you're not supposed to be organized and you respect the other person's style.

We learned from their tribal nature. A sense of humor ran through everything that the Kesey people did. They had a rollicking, good-natured, hit-the-road quality that we needed. We learned from that.

At the end of the journey, Kesey is cornered by a reporter from the New York *Herald Tribune*. As the Pranksters play ball on the green lawn of Central Park (except for Cassady, that is, who is talking-up a couple of secretaries from Viking Press), Kesey explains the purpose of the trip to the puzzled journalist, in this archival transcription by Ken Babbs:

QUESTION: What was the genesis of the trip?
KEN KESEY: For a lot of us it started when we first read *On the Road*. That's why it's so beautiful that we have Cassady driving. This is like a cub scout's dream. Viking wanted me here to do the publicity thing, which is generally uncomfortable. Babbs and I were going to come out in his Volkswagen and then other friends started coming and it snowballed into what it is now.

QUESTION: This trip seems to be without ulterior motives. On the other hand you're making tape recordings and filming. Is this for possible future work?
KEN KESEY: Like my dad used to say, "You have to take your fishing pole into the woods, otherwise people think you're crazy walking up and down the creek." Those tape recorders and cameras have gone a long way toward making us *responsible*. Able to respond. Able to see. We had a scene in Wikieup, Arizona. We had been travelling a long time and it was

(OPPOSITE PAGE) MILLBROOK RESIDENT SUSAN METZNER GIVING NEAL CASSADY A SHOT OF DMT.
(ALLEN GINSBERG)

NEAL CASSADY AFTER A DMT INJECTION, WITH NURSE/GUIDE SUSAN METZNER, IN THE ATTIC OF THE MILLBROOK MANSION.
(ALLEN GINSBERG)

hot, and we had been hot a long time, and we were looking for the cool place. We found a cattle bog with water about three feet deep, and it was cool and clear and there was a space about a hundred yards long to drive the bus across.

So it looked good to me, and we got out halfways and down the bus went. Stuck to the axles. So Dale went off on our motorcycle to get a tractor. We hooked up to it and this farmer was just flabbergasted at the whole scene—everyone was running around making a lot of fuss—and there was a lot of furor of digging around the wheels, and Dale was trying to put the motorcycle back on the back of the bus, and I saw that although we had three cameras working, two of them weren't even being used. The operators were so interested in what was going on that they were watching instead of filming. The third camera—the guy with the beard, Zonk—was taking pictures of the beautiful scenery. The clouds. The trees. I flipped. I jumped up on top of the motorcycle up on the bus and hollered, "You idiots! This stuck bus is what's happening. Not that scenery. Get over here and film us getting unstuck."

When I do this—record what's going on without making a judgment out of it—something happens to me. I get back to being myself. I feel like I'm working on all cylinders again. Instead of drawing that moon that's really there in a kitchen on paper mills, I'm shooting the fingernails that are crawling out of the mire.

QUESTION: I have gone out on tours with movie companies that seemed to be mostly pretense. This seems to be mostly reality.

KEN KESEY: We are trying to pretend that we are not pretending. We go someplace. We put on our show. Babbs struts around. He's the blustery, big-mouthed Marine. We have this camaraderie we've built up. Working not to deny anything. Cassady and George Walker both drive the bus well. But they drive entirely different. Cassady drives for the excitement. He's W.C. Fields and he loves it. He'd rather do it than anything—bounce around and make a lot of noise.

George is calm and can shift without a gear smash. And between them, who are the closest actually, there's the most sparks. So when Cassady drives, George comes up and sits behind him and Cassady goes into third gear mania. He can't get the bus into third gear. Then he fumes at somebody, usually George.

QUESTION: Is there any taking of sides by the others when something like this happens?

KEN KESEY: No. We work it in to where it's just part of the show. Babbs will come storming forth saying, "Come on, y'all. Do the Merry Pranksters fall apart in this fashion?" And we will fume, but it's hard to know anyway if what you're doing is real or if it's acting. I don't even think it's necessary that you should know. We all play our roles. Talking on a leash, that's the kind of role I play. It's been as crazy an experience as I have had.

QUESTION: In general, has the attitude of the public been friendly or hostile?

KEN KESEY: Completely friendly. Children in particular. Children understand, you can see it in their faces. If you were a kid standing out on the street and suddenly here comes a brightly colored bus with a bunch of clowny people making a lot of noise, you can guess the reaction. We saw a guy when we first came into New York, a ninety-year-old man—a grotesque man—with a little transistor radio he was holding in his hand, and when he saw us coming by he goes, "ARGGHH! ARGGHH! ARGGHH!" And it was a wonderful sign of recognition.

When we came to New York, going full tilt with our generator roaring and sound on the top and the bottom of the bus, I began to think, "Maybe this is it, this is all it's ever to be. Whatever it is we've put together, right here is where it's happening." We were operating at peak efficiency. We played to an enormous audience. We played briefly to each person and then moved on to another one. It was a lot of fun. But that may be it. It may go on and something else happen to it, but I don't know.

We've got all this film that I still have hopes for. I think that if we have anything at all with the film it should be a pretty accurate report of a learning process.

(OPPOSITE PAGE) TIM LEARY STANDS NEAR THE WINDOW OF HIS THIRD-FLOOR STUDY. ON THE FRONT OF THE MANSION IS A PAINTING OF "TURNED-ON MAN." (UPI/BETTMANN NEWSPHOTOS)

KESEY HOLDS FORTH AT A STRATEGY SESSION PRIOR TO THE 1966 ACID TEST GRADUATION. (TED STRESHINSKY)

The Acid Tests — and Beyond

By the end of August 1964, these astronauts of inner space had returned to La Honda, their Bay Area home base. The scene around La Honda was expanding, with more Pranksters and would-be Pranksters showing up all the time.

Mountain Girl was there when the bus returned. She had gone to a birthday party for Neal Cassady, who had returned from New York with Hassler, ahead of the others. She was a big, loud, lusty, eighteen-year-old from upstate New York with a black motorcycle and an engaging manner. Her name was Carolyn Adams, but Cassady dubbed her "Mountain Girl," and convinced her that the *real* bohemian lifestyle she was looking for on the West Coast was up at a place in La Honda that was manned by the crew of a wildly painted school bus.

She fit in like she had been a Prankster all along. Kesey took to her right away, and soon developed a lifelong friendship with her. She had a daughter (Sunshine) with Kesey and is now married to Jerry Garcia, guitarist for the Grateful Dead.

Cassady also introduced a Nordic-looking blonde who was dubbed "June the Goon," because she constantly talked about psychological hang-ups. Page Browning was living there in a tent back up in the redwoods. Ron Boise, the hard-drinking metal sculptor, was welding car bodies into the sexual positions of the *Kamasutra*.

Lee Quarnstrom was working as a reporter for the *San Mateo Times* and came up to do a story on Kesey. He fell in love with the scene and quit the newspaper to become a sort of minister of information.

The counterculture was growing all over the country. College students were rejecting the system and were taking a stand against the Vietnam War, racism, and sexual repression; and they were united by desires to foster peace, understanding, free love, and freedom to experiment.

"It was the use of acid that just opened the whole scene into relative reality," says Ram Dass. "What Einstein did to Newtonian physics, [acid] did to social consciousness. LSD said, 'You think this is real, but it's only relatively real.' The effect was incredible. It was carried by the rock movement, by rock lyrics, and it permeated the culture with sexual freedom, gay rights, and minority uprising. It went on and on."

"The rule was 'Never trust a Prankster,'" says Lee Quarnstrom. "It was that way because you could never really trust any of us. Rather than have to explain something like why we ate all the food in Gordon Lish's refrigerator and left no note or explanation, you could just say, 'Never trust a Prankster.'" It was another case of the Pranksters meeting rational expectations (of morality, of controlled behavior) with illogic. For Ken Babbs, the reason you should never trust a Prankster is the same reason you shouldn't expect perfection from non-Pranksters: people are human.

The Pranksters spent their days using LSD, mingling with the curious, talking philosophy, hanging out, and, of course, editing mountains of film. Forty-five hours of home movies, the world's first acid film—as Kesey saw it, a *cinema* novel—a film that would have at least the impact of his books. He was going to pioneer a new medium.

Word of mouth was painting Kesey as a full-blown counterculture hero. After all, here was an internationally acclaimed novelist who had put aside writing and the novel form—*the old way of doing things*—and bet everything he had on a new way of looking at things—*movies*. And he did not exactly hoard the money that came his way. The film and processing alone cost Kesey $70,000. Add to that another $33,000 for living expenses and, by the end of 1965, Kesey had spend $103,000 of his own money on the movie.

But there were problems with the film. Some footage was out of focus or shot with a jiggling camera. Scenes were over- or under-exposed. Ron Bevirt says that the central problems that made it difficult to shape the movie into a theatrical release were the absence of establishing shots that would give the scenes a story context or sense of significance, and the lack of a plot. "It was little snippets, vignettes, and there was never a possibility of making it into a unified whole," he says.

They tried to get it into shape, editing constantly and showing what they had edited to everyone who crossed the bridge. Hunter S. Thompson talks of twenty hours of film being shown during which Kesey tried to convince him to drop journalism and go into filmmaking.

JERRY GARCIA, MOP IN HAND, WALKING ON ASHBURY STREET IN SAN FRANCISCO IN 1966. (GENE ANTHONY)

JOURNALIST HUNTER THOMPSON, WHO INTRODUCED KESEY AND THE PRANKSTERS TO THE HELL'S ANGELS: "I DIDN'T KNOW HOW [THE ANGELS] WOULD TAKE TO KESEY BECAUSE THEY DIDN'T KNOW HIM FROM SHIT. BUT THEY TOOK TO HIM RIGHT AWAY. IT WAS LIKE I'D BROUGHT THEM BOB DYLAN. WE SMOKED A COUPLE OF JOINTS AND THEY JUST LIKED HIM. IT WAS A LOVE AFFAIR RIGHT FROM THE START." (*NEWSWEEK*-WALLY MCNAMEE)

"He was so convincing at times that I was almost ready to stop writing," says Thompson. "Then I watched about twenty hours of their films. . . . I'm glad he's writing again, because he wasn't a great filmmaker."

The film, the acid, the excitement and novelty of their activities, and Kesey's charisma drew more and more people. The members of the Grateful Dead (who were then known as the Warlocks), Allen Ginsberg, Owsley the acid manufacturer, academics from Stanford, writers, drifters, and, also, the police, all came to visit. Although LSD still was legal, the crowd at La Honda was freely using marijuana and other drugs which *were* illegal. On April 23, 1965, the police crossed the bridge with seventeen deputies, eight police dogs, and a federal agent named Willie Wong who was carrying a search warrant.

Most of the Pranksters were arrested, but after months of fighting legal battles, including fifteen court appearances, charges were dropped against everybody except Kesey and Page Browning, who only ended up being charged on one count of "possession of marijuana."

During all of this the Prankster party seemed to expand to cover all of San Francisco. A counterculture was developing. By 1967, be-ins filled Golden Gate Park, drug use increased, the anti-war movement grew in intensity, and rock music found an offshoot known as "acid rock," shaped by the firsthand acid experience of the Grateful Dead and other San Francisco groups, like the Jefferson Airplane, and Country Joe and the Fish.

The Merry Pranksters Meet the Hell's Angels

It was also during this period that Kesey met the Hell's Angels through "gonzo" journalist Hunter Thompson, who was writing his classic *Hell's Angels: The Strange and Terrible Saga of the Outlaw Motorcycle Gangs*. Although Thompson tried to persuade Kesey to leave them alone, Kesey invited them to his place in La Honda for a good old-fashioned picnic attended by Allen Ginsberg, Ram Dass, and the Merry Pranksters, among others. The party went on for two days and involved at least one extended raunchy episode, but no savage brutality—much to the relief of the police holding a vigil on the other side of the bridge.

"I was totally wrong about acid and the Angels," says Thompson. "I thought it would bring out the worst in them but it didn't."

When Thompson saw the Angels earnestly studying Allen Ginsberg's performance of Hindu chants accompanied by finger cymbals, he rethought his aversion to acid. It didn't just unleash inhibitions and allow mayhem to surface. Thompson had been told that his own nature was truly violent and this had always made him avoid the drug. But since it didn't seem to rile even the Hell's Angels, he cast aside his caution and took his first hit that weekend. He'd never forget his motorcycle ride home.

The Acid Tests

Kesey had been planning a geodesic dome with a foam rubber floor. People could lie down, take acid, and watch a light show or the bus movie projected on the ceiling, or listen to music or tapes of the bus trip. *Turn on, tune in, drop out.*

"Roy Sebern did one of the first light shows," says Babbs. "He had an overhead projector and he got a bug and put it on the tray. And this bug was just huge up there on the wall. Then he put a spider on the tray, and these two things fought. I'll never forget it. It was one of the best shows I've ever seen."

"THE INTREPID TRAVELLER," KEN BABBS. "NEVER TRUST A PRANKSTER," WAS ONE OF THE SAYINGS THAT THE PRANKSTERS COINED. BABBS SAYS THAT THE REASON FOR NEVER TRUSTING PRANKSTERS IS THAT THEY ARE HUMAN JUST LIKE ANYONE ELSE. ACCORDING TO LEE QUARNSTROM, THIS RULE CAME IN HANDY WHEN HAVING TO EXPLAIN WHY, FOR INSTANCE, PRANKSTERS ATE ALL THE FOOD IN GORDON LISH'S REFRIGERATOR AND LEFT NO NOTE. (RON BEVIRT)

The weekend gatherings were getting too big to be held in anyone's house. The Pranksters decided to move the weekend showings to Babbs's place in Santa Cruz, a chicken ranch gone to seed known as "the Spread."

The Grateful Dead—Garcia, Pigpen, Phil Lesh, Bob Weir, and Bill Kreutzmann—set up in the living room and played. The Pranksters joined in. Ginsberg chanted. Kesey and Babbs were there, and Cassady rapped into a microphone. At dawn everyone left. It was the first Acid Test.

The second Acid Test happened on December 4, 1965, in San Jose, on the night of a Rolling Stones concert. At the concert, the Pranksters passed out crayon-lettered handbills for a house party. Their cryptic message was a street address and the words: "Can YOU Pass the Acid Test?" About 300 to 400 people showed up and the Grateful Dead played until the police broke up the party.

Acid Test three was held at Muir Beach, a state park about ten miles north of San Francisco. It was a perfect setting: an empty winter beach, a huge empty log lodge, and no police. They had all gone further north to Stinson Beach, where the Acid Test was originally scheduled to be held.

About 300 people watched the bus movie, and took in Roy Sebern's light show and music by the Grateful Dead.

A good stone was had by all, except Kesey. At dawn he told the other Pranksters that the Acid Tests were over. Too many people, too much weird energy, too many bad vibes. No more, said the Chief.

Kesey Is Busted and Heads for Mexico

But the Acid Tests continued anyway. Stewart Brand, a biologist with an interest in Indian peyote cults, organized the "Trips Festival," a three-night celebration that would include Kesey and the Merry Pranksters the second night.

A couple of nights before the Trips Festival, while sitting on the roof of Stewart Brand's apartment building in North Beach, Kesey and Mountain Girl were busted for possession of marijuana. This was Kesey's second bust, which was not a good thing to have in 1966. It carried a stiff jail sentence which Kesey, as a highly visible public figure, could not expect to avoid.

Some of the Pranksters think he tried to get busted, for one reason or another. If he wasn't trying to get arrested, he certainly did not go out of his way to avoid it. Frequently he appeared in public in spite of his fugitive status, going to movies, appearing as a guest lecturer in Ed McClanahan's writing class, and even going so far as to appear on television.

"I think Ken had a fascination with the underside of society, with the rebellious of society," says Ram Dass, in retrospect. "I think he had a tremendous amount of anger in him at the time."

And so the legal problems increased for Kesey.

After the Trips Festival a warrant for his arrest was issued, and he didn't cotton to the idea of spending a couple of years in the San Mateo County jail. Mexico was the answer. As Kesey is quoted as saying in *The Electric Kool-Aid Acid Test*: "If society wants me to be an outlaw, then I'll be an outlaw and a damned good one. That's something people need. People at all times need outlaws."

Off he went, but not until he staged his own suicide. He wrote a suicide note and gave it to his cousin Dale. Dale drove an old panel truck up the coast, parked it near the cliffs overlooking the ocean, and put the note on the dashboard. According to plan, everyone was supposed to think that Kesey had killed himself.

But things didn't work out exactly as planned.

The Pranksters Carry On

With Kesey in Mexico, Babbs was the man in charge. He took the bus to Los Angeles for a series of Acid Tests. With the help of Wavy Gravy (also known as Hugh Romney), the Pranksters put on four Acid Tests. The first was in a Unitarian Church in Northridge, a dome-shaped edifice where dozens of acid heads and a few rank-and-file Unitarians showed up to drop acid and eat Prankster-prepared pineapple chili. Like ministers, Cassady and Wavy Gravy stood before the assembled multitude rapping to each other over microphones. It was later described as a sort of mind reading experience, in which Cassady knew what Wavy was going to say before he said it. At the time it must have seemed a bit like the Synched-up Church of the Acid Sacrament.

From there they moved into Watts, which was still figuratively smoldering after the Watts Riots of 1966. They rented a warehouse and announced the Test in the Los Angeles *Free Press* and over the radio. Films were shown, Kool-Aid was served and the Grateful Dead played amidst light shows and Hassler's slide show of wild flowers.

The police were there, but, not knowing what to do, they just took in the scene as straight observers. Acid was still legal at this point, but a bill making LSD a controlled substance had been passed in the California Legislature, and would go into effect on October 6, 1966. This date led some of the mystically inclined to attach an ironic biblical significance to its triple sixes—the mark of the antichrist in the Book of Revelations. The half-serious implication among the heads was that the State of California was assuming the role of the devil in keeping people from "seeing God."

Another Test was held in a warehouse in Hollywood; then the L.A. Acid Tests came to an end. They did one more in an old Hollywood sound studio, but life just wasn't the same without Kesey. And besides, being an acid messiah is hard work. As Ron Bevirt explains: "People

FAYE AND KEN KESEY
AT THE ACID TEST
GRADUATION.
(TED STRESHINSKY)

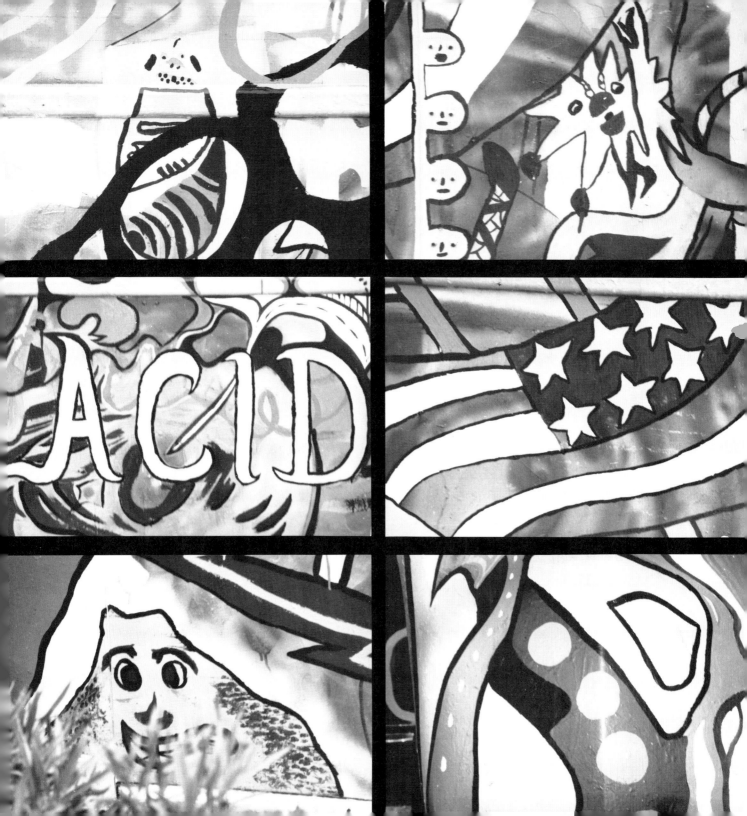

didn't realize how tough it is to take LSD. It wears you out. But to put on an event, tear down and clean it up, to lead a group of people looking for enlightenment is even tougher. It exhausted us."

The media were catching on that something newsworthy was happening. *Life* wanted to put them on the cover, said photographer Lawrence Schiller. He convinced the Pranksters to drive the bus over to a big photo studio, where he invited them in for a photo session.

As Schiller photographed the Pranksters, Babbs loaded up a very pregnant Mountain Girl, Zonker, George Walker, and some of the others, and left. Babbs had pranked the Pranksters—including Cassady, and off they went, with the bus and a scaled-down crew, to Mexico. Other Pranksters followed later.

. . .

This section features a number of photographs taken at the "Acid Test Graduation" in San Francisco on October 31, 1966. According to *The Electric Kool-Aid Acid Test,* this event took place shortly after Kesey came back to the United States after his sojourn in Mexico. In interviews in the San Francisco *Chronicle* and in two television interviews Kesey delared his intention to remain a fugitive, "as salt in J. Edgar Hoover's wounds."

The Pranksters planned a Trips Festival which would showcase a grand act of defiance by Kesey. The plan was for Kesey to emerge from hiding, unmask himself, and deliver a sermon about the need of the psychedelic community to go "beyond acid." The police would undoubtedly close in, at which point Kesey would ascend a rope to a trap door in the roof and take off in a waiting helicopter, piloted by Ken Babbs.

The full execution of this particular fantasy/plan was prevented by Kesey's arrest on the Harbor Freeway on October 20. But after his release on bail, he did take part in the Acid Test Graduation, declaring his candidacy for the Governorship of California and counselling the acid community to go beyond the "Garden of Eden" and "Innocence" of acid. It proved to be the end of the acid test era. Weeks later, Kesey faced the first of two jury trials which ultimately resulted in his being sentenced to a prison work farm. On his release, he returned to Oregon, as did a number of the Pranksters.

(OPPOSITE PAGE) ACID TEST-ERA BUS PAINTING DETAILS. (RON BEVIRT)

THE ACID TESTS — AND BEYOND
— ORAL HISTORIES . . .

(OPPOSITE PAGE) NEAL CASSADY WITH HIS EVER-PRESENT HAMMER IN FRONT OF THE CONDEMNED RENO HOTEL IN SAN FRANCISCO. AS DESCRIBED IN *THE ELECTRIC KOOL-AID ACID TEST*: "HE SEEMS TO BE IN A KINETIC TRANCE, FLIPPING A SMALL SLEDGE HAMMER UP IN THE AIR OVER AND OVER, ALWAYS MANAGING TO CATCH THE HANDLE ON THE WAY DOWN." (TED STRESHINSKY)

. . . in which an expanded band of Merry Pranksters commence a series of events in amplified-sound wired, colored-electric-light lit, semi-public places designed for groups of people to take LSD together and experience whatever results. . . .

Journalist Hunter S. Thompson introduces Kesey to members of the infamous motorcycle gang, the Hell's Angels, and as the Angels and Kesey discover their mutual regard, Kesey invites them to his home to meet the Pranksters and receive an initiation into the cult of psychedelics. . . .

An alliance is formed between the Hell's Angels and the Merry Pranksters which disintegrates, according to Thompson, when Kesey and Ginsberg encourage them to join Berkeley anti-war protesters in a confrontation with Oakland police. Angels fight both police and leftists, and relations with the Angels go "to hell after that". . .

As a counterculture blooms in San Francisco, drawing people from all over the country, Acid Tests evolve into mass rallies like the "Be-ins" in Golden Gate Park, and the Trips Festival at the Longshoremen's Hall. Law-enforcement authorities take a growing, particular interest in Kesey and the Pranksters, frequently scrutinizing their homes, and their persons at events where people can be seen taking a raucous and inordinate interest in perception. Kesey and the Pranksters are ticketed for operating a vehicle with a bent license plate and arrested for possessing small quantities of marijuana, the most serious charge available to police since possession of LSD was legal until October 6, 1966. . . .

After a second marijuana-possession arrest, which was certain to draw a prison sentence, Kesey stages a fake suicide and flees across California's southern border into Mexico. . . .

The Pranksters' Acid Tests continue during Kesey's exile and extend from San Francisco to Los Angeles; then they take the bus south and join him. . . .

In Mexico, real and imagined Mexican police and FBI agents trail Kesey. Pranksters Zonker and Hassler are involved in an auto accident. Mountain Girl has a baby. Kesey reenters the U.S. on horseback, disguised as a drunken singing cowboy. He appears in public and is eventually arrested and sent to prison. On his release, he returns to Oregon, where he remains to this day.

This section features commentary from: Lee Quarnstrom, Ron Bevirt, Ed McClanahan, Baba Ram Dass, Allen Ginsberg, Ken Babbs, Steve Lambrecht, Robert Stone, Timothy Leary, and:

WAVY GRAVY—standup comedian and performer, who is also known to friends as Hugh Romney.

DENISE KAUFMANN—a.k.a. "Mary Microgram," who was a member of the band "Ace of Cups," in addition to being a Prankster.

HUNTER THOMPSON—who was at the beginning of his writing career in 1965, when he introduced the Hell's Angels to Kesey and the Pranksters.

LEE QUARNSTROM: I was involved in the Acid Tests from the beginning.

They were really an extension of some of the things we were doing in La Honda. There was a little amphitheater up behind the house. Kesey had the whole place wired with loudspeakers and earphones and lights and things. Artsy people called them "Happenings," but they were just a way of extending to other people what we had done in the privacy of our own bus.

PAGE BROWNING IN CALIFORNIA, PLAYING PICCOLO FOR THE PRANKSTERS' MOVIE, SOUND BEING PICKED UP BY A MOVIE SOUND BOOM. (RON BEVIRT)

JERRY GARCIA AND PIGPEN
PLAYING AT STEWART BRAND'S
"WHAT'S HAPPENING" EVENT,
HELD AT SAN FRANCISCO STATE
UNIVERSITY IN 1966.
(RON BEVIRT)

For instance, there was "The Power Game." We had this spinner that would be spun around and whoever it pointed to would get all the power for the next half-hour. They could use it or abuse it. They could say, "We're all gonna clean my car," or they could just walk around and have everyone follow them. It was a particular high to have twenty people staring into your eyes for thirty minutes. It was Kesey's way of being psychedelic without drugs.

RON BEVIRT: At La Honda we had regular Saturday night parties that we got ready for all week by hanging lights, putting up various kinds of decor, and setting the stage. We were also editing film and sound tape for the movie. Then at some point we ventured forth into public venues.

Later we got involved with the Hell's Angels, and they came down and partied with us at La Honda. We went to Muir Beach and did an Acid Test there. We did an Acid Test in Palo Alto. We did an Acid Test in San Jose. We did one in the Fillmore Auditorium. We did the Longshoremen's Hall Trips Festival and then we did the "What's Happening" thing at San Francisco State University. Basically, those were the Acid Tests we did in northern California.

LEE QUARNSTROM: I went down to La Honda and did a story that was a combination review/interview. I was taken in by La Honda and by Kesey, and decided to rent a house not far from Kesey's. Eventually, I just quit my job at the *San Mateo Times* and got involved in full-time pranking.

The word "charismatic" is overused but Kesey is truly one of the few people I've ever met who can really command attention. He is so charming and seductive and has such flashes of brilliance that you can't help but be overwhelmed by him.

ED MCCLANAHAN: I don't recall that he was writing anything at all after the bus trip. The scene made you feel like literature or literary conversation was passe, and not really anything that anybody in his right mind would waste too much time on.

KEN BABBS: That's probably because Kesey's mind was on a different medium—film. Time was being spent trying to make sense of the 45 hours of film that had been shot on the bus trip. Not only were we tripping on acid, but we were tripping on film, too.

ED MCCLANAHAN: I remember the first year they were back; they all went away for Christmas. I stopped in at the La Honda house one day when there wasn't a soul there, except Page Browning. Page was always around; he was just basically living full-time at La Honda.

They had a gigantic Christmas tree in the living room of that old house and it was decorated with film. It was totally enshrouded in endless reels of exposed film. I don't know if it was from the cutting room floor or what, but there was a barrel of it.

Wavy Gravy discovered LSD while he was Tom Wolfe's roommate in New York. In San Francisco, he became an "acid businessman," dealing LSD (which was legal then) part-time and performing his comedy routine at night. Across the Bay, in Berkeley, Denise Kaufmann had just enrolled in the University of California, where she discovered LSD and the free-speech movement within a few days of each other. One of her sources for acid was Augustus Owsley Stanley III, or just "Owsley," a Berkeley chemistry major who mass-produced high-quality acid. He was dubbed "the unofficial Mayor of San Francisco," by the Haight-Ashbury crowd for manufacturing the purest acid known to the Haight.

WAVY GRAVY: The path that led me to the Acid Tests started about 1960 in New York City. I had gone to acting school at the Neighborhood Playhouse. In the evenings after class, I would read my poetry in the coffee houses of Greenwich Village. For a while, people would line up four deep around the block to see the Beatniks. It was kind of a geek show, but it provided ample material.

In between poems I began to improvise, talking about the strange things that occurred in my life. Finally Lenny Bruce saw me improvising and said, "Skip the poetry." He became my manager. He started mailing me around the country so I could tell about the strange events in my life and the little head riffs that came up in the abnormal course of thought. The next thing I knew, I was opening for John Coltrane, and Thelonious Monk. At the same time, I shared a room above the Gaslight with Bob Dylan and got to know the people in the folk revival real intimately. Meanwhile, my comedy—or whatever it was—got stranger and stranger.

DENISE KAUFMANN: I met Kesey and the Pranksters quite a while before the first Acid Tests. They had just come back from going across country, and I was a student at Berkeley. I was standing out in front

PRANKSTER DENISE KAUFMANN— "MARY MICROGRAM"—WHO HAD A BAND CALLED THE ACE OF CUPS: "ABOUT A WEEK AFTER MEETING KESEY, HE SHOWED UP AT MY APARTMENT IN BERKELEY AND SAID, 'I'VE COME TO GET YOU. PACK. COME AND LIVE WITH US AT THE FARM.' AND I DID IT. A MAJOR LIFE DECISION IN ONE SECOND. THAT'S HOW I GOT INVOLVED IN THE ACID TESTS." (RON BEVIRT)

of Sproul Hall where people had all those tables with different information about the Communist party and the Socialists. And while I was standing there, the police came and took the people away. The guy next to me was Mario Savio [founder of the Berkeley Free Speech Movement], so I like to say that I was right there when the free-speech movement started. I was beaten up and arrested at Sproul Hall, which was really an eye opener for this little Jewish girl from San Francisco.

WAVY GRAVY: I abandoned the MacDougal Street scene and put together a show that I thought was unique—myself, Tiny Tim, and Moon Dog. We opened at the Fat Black Pussycat Cafe and Theatre, and got rave reviews the next day in the *Village Voice*. The only problem was that the theater was closed after our first show by tax people, so there was no one inside to answer the phone, which was ringing off the hook because of the review. Since no one was there, the three of us started calling ourselves "The Phantom Cabaret."

Around this time I had my first psychedelic experience. I took mescaline on Coney Island and bought $50 worth of roller coaster tickets. I remember it got scary every time I got off the roller coaster, and I've been fairly strange ever since.

I married a French girl at the Gaslight, with Bobby Dylan and Tom Paxton there in the audience, and we left for the West Coast to help Lenny Bruce, who was having legal battles over some problems about his ability to perform without legal harassment.

DENISE KAUFMANN: I didn't come from a radical background, but toward the end of that year I met a whole lot of people who were way outside the realm of anybody that I had known, including some people who were taking LSD. Berkeley was also where music became my passion. I got into a band and started taking LSD all in the spring of that year. We had this particular incident where we took some LSD and went to the Greek Theatre at Berkeley that night. There I had this experience that was definitely unexplainable. It was almost as though we changed our vibratory rate, or something. We went from being solid mass to being some other form of energy.

I was up on the stage and very high on acid. From the stage there's a drop down that was maybe eight feet. I was on stage and I walked right out into the air. At some point, as I was walking on air, I thought, "You are walking on air," at which point I fell, face down.

I knew I had broken my face. My boyfriend was there and we were both aware that I had done horrible damage to myself.

I can't describe exactly what we did after that, but we were both aware of slowing down the energy so that it was a melding and healing process. It's hard to talk about it because I don't really understand it.

I know I looked really scary so we decided at about sunrise that I should go to the hospital. We walked into the emergency room and people just said, "Oh God." They took me in and did X-rays. Then they called me back in and did another set of X-rays. Then they did a third set of X-rays and finally said "Look, we can tell by the way the blood is clotted on your

CAROLYN ADAMS—"MOUNTAIN GIRL." (RON BEVIRT)

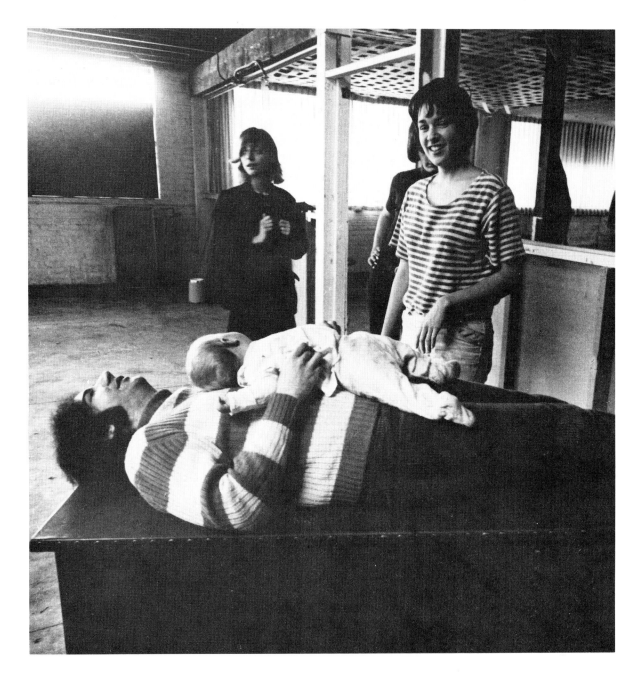

AS HER MOTHER, MOUNTAIN GIRL, LOOKS ON, SUNSHINE RESTS ON TOP OF JERRY GARCIA DURING A BREAK AT THE DEAD'S PRACTICE STUDIO, "THE HELIPORT," IN SAUSALITO. LEE QUARNSTROM RELATES DETAILS OF HER NAMING DURING THE PRANKSTERS' MEXICAN EXILE: "THEY WANTED TO NAME HER SUNSHINE, AS SHE'S KNOWN TODAY, BUT WHEN THEY REGISTERED AT CITY HALL, SOMEBODY WHO THOUGHT THEY SPOKE SPANISH GAVE HER NAME AS *SOLANA* OR *SOLANO* — MY RECOLLECTION IS THAT THAT TURNED OUT TO MEAN 'SUN PORCH.'" (GENE ANTHONY)

face that it looks like you have broken bones. But we don't see any sign of it on the X-rays. We can't explain it."

I told them, "Don't try to explain it," and we left. My boyfriend and I didn't talk. When we reached the sidewalk, he went one way and I went the other. We just had no place to put this experience.

Acid use was covering the Bay Area like a fog, engulfing people who normally would not have exposed themselves to a drug that dissected their egos like LSD. After all, there is an enormous difference between mind drugs and body drugs, especially when you consider that mind drugs can open closets filled with psychological skeletons too horrible for many to look at. This is precisely why Hunter Thompson didn't want Kesey to introduce the Hell's Angels to LSD. Thompson was working on a book about the Angels, and thought he knew them well enough to understand how they would react to LSD.

HUNTER THOMPSON: Kesey and I had been on an afternoon television program at KQED, the Public Broadcasting station in San Francisco. The one reason I went was because Kesey was going to be there. It was three in the afternoon and the subject was: "What is the free speech movement?"

After the show we went with the director of the program to some bar down on Mission, and drank and had a good time talking.

Suddenly I realized that it was close to five o'clock and I had to return a record album to a Hell's Angel named Frenchy down at Hunter's Point. We had been talking about the Angels so Kesey said, "What the hell, let's all go see these guys." Curiosity makes for all the problems in the world.

I had written an article for *The Nation* magazine about the Hell's Angels, so I was OK with them. But I didn't know how they would take to Kesey, because they didn't know him from shit. But they took to him right away. It was like I'd brought them Bob Dylan. We smoked a couple of joints and they just liked him. It was a love affair from the start.

RAM DASS: I think Kesey got involved with the Angels because there was a tremendous amount of theater to them. There was a harshness about them and an innocent animal quality. Later they became pretty crude, but early on they were like, well, dirty angels.

This is what Kesey had a fascination with: they were the underside of society, the disenfranchised who were rebelling with anger.

Just like the Rolling Stones and the Grateful Dead later used the Angels, Kesey wanted to have an alliance with such anti-social elements so he could use them as security guards.

The Angels accepted Kesey's invitation and came down to La Honda to meet the Pranksters. The date was August 7, 1965. The Pranksters had spiffed up the house in preparation for the outlaw motorcycle gang's arrival. Music was blasting, food was cooking, and acid was already being circulated among the Pranksters and the other guests, who included Allen Ginsberg, Ram Dass, Ed McClanahan and a couple dozen others. A sign was hung across the bridge leading to the house, fifteen-feet long and three-feet high: THE MERRY PRANKSTERS WELCOME THE HELL'S ANGELS.

Four police cars lined the road, waiting for the riot that was sure to come. Then up the road came forty Harley-Davidsons; the party was about to begin.

ALLEN GINSBERG:

First Party at Ken Kesey's With Hell's Angels

Cool black night thru the redwoods
cars parked outside in shade
behind the gate, stars dim above
the ravine, a fire burning by the side
porch and a few tired souls hunched over
in black leather jackets. In the huge
wooden house, a yellow chandelier
at 3 a.m. the blast of loudspeakers
hi-fi Rolling Stones Ray Charles Beatles
Jumping Joe Jackson and twenty youths
dancing to the vibration thru the floor,
a little weed in the bathroom, girls in scarlet
tights, one muscular smooth skinned man
sweating dancing for hours, beer cans
bent littering the yard, a hanged man
sculpture dangling from a high creek branch,
children sleeping softly in their bedroom bunks.
And 4 police cars parked outside the painted
gate, red lights revolving in the leaves

December 1965

HUNTER THOMPSON: I was opposed to the weekend foray in La Honda. When we left the Angel hangout I told Kesey, "You motherfucking, crazy bastard, you'll pay for this from Maine to here." I was opposed to it. Maybe, in fact, I felt responsible.

I thought they would take the Pranksters apart like cooked chicken. I had been [to La Honda] and knew that it was a gang of innocents playing with fire.

The Angels were into speed, downers, and other body drugs. I was afraid that acid would make the Angels far too violent.

I had never taken acid. I had been told that I was far too violent to do acid. I ran into acid in 1960 in Big Sur, when I was around Michael Murphy

at Esalen. When he said that I would be far too violent to do acid I figured, well, if it's that crazy, I shouldn't run the risk, you know, of going nuts, getting violent. Michael thought I was a violent person and so did I. I was concerned about what I had set in motion. And worst of all, I had jumped into politics instead of journalism.

RON BEVIRT: None of us really knew what to expect. We were all as nervous as hell, but Kesey said everything would be okay so we just trusted him. We cleaned house and made the big welcome banner and then we just waited. Remember, the Hell's Angels didn't have a great reputation.

KEN BABBS: Instead of fighting the Hell's Angels, or being afraid of them, we managed to absorb them. I think it had to do with the psychedelic expansion of consciousness. The Angels were surrounded with people who could be very peaceful, loving people, whose best natures were coming out, and who were learning to move and dance in crowds without creating any hostility or bummer vibes.

It was the actual thing of finding the cool spot in everybody and letting that come out, rather than searching for the hot spot and pushing the anger button. The movie's title, *The Merry Pranksters Search for the Cool Place*, refers to this—the cool place inside of people.

HUNTER THOMPSON: When the Angels went down to La Honda I figured I had to go. What the hell? I remember the Angels coming down the road from the little village of La Honda. Mountain Girl really tried to gussy the place up for the new guests.

All in all, it was so naive that I was terrified. But the first night was a great victory for Kesey because he kept it nonviolent. The Angels took to acid quick, too quick for me as I recall. I was still trying to referee a little bit. You know, "No, Neal, don't give him that. No, stay away Terry [the Tramp], that's not for you." I figured if it was too violent for me then it was way too violent for them.

But it got away from me pretty quickly. After all, the Angels were curious, too. I could see what was happening: Angels were falling over. Terry the Tramp walked up to me, suddenly convinced that he had been turned into a rooster and would be killed and cooked the minute the meeting stopped. So every time there would be a break in the music—which was coming from speakers hidden in all the trees—Terry would run and hide. People were going out of control left and right and I could see that this was going to be a long night.

When I realized it had gotten away from me, Ken offered me some acid. I said, "Alright, fuck this," and ate the stuff. He gave me about 400 mics. I kept waiting for terrible things to happen and they didn't. It was a victory for the acid, really. I had a wonderful time. It was at least two-and-a-half days later before I got back to town.

The whole thing turned out to be a massive crossing of lines.

There were a few lines that were crossed over, too. A friend of the Pranksters offered to have sex with a line-up of Hell's Angels and an eerie scene resulted.

RAM DASS: I was there in the room. I remember it so well, because many of the Angels were too stoned to get erections. There must have been twenty guys in the room and this one girl, and they were all around her with their pants down playing with their cocks, and one guy was on top of her and he couldn't get an erection.

RON BEVIRT: The Angels were very courtly. They were calling the woman "ma'am." Ram Dass and I were just sitting against the wall watching this scene. This one Angel was having a terrible time getting an erection. He was playing with himself and feeling the woman, but nothing was working. Finally he said, "Maybe things would go better if the people who weren't participating would leave." Ram Dass and I exited.

HUNTER THOMPSON: She was not struggling in any way. It was ceremonial.

There were people I didn't know who finally got into it. I think under the circumstances she could have left any time she wanted to because the Angels would have been way out of line if they said, "No, you can't leave." They did create the atmosphere, but then so did she.

I was astounded, though, when they brought Neal into the room. He was a friend of hers and I thought when he came in there that he'd flip out. It worried me and I wanted to leave, but I was a writer and it wasn't something I could ignore. As it was, he seemed to accept it very well. I remember her kissing him when he said, "Kiss me," and then *he* fucked her. I've never said this before, but it's true.

I have a weird memory for that stuff and I can still see it. At any given time there were twenty people in the room and maybe half of those either participating or likely to. There were always four or five participating, sort of like a bunch of cats toying with a mouse. Word of it seeped out, and pretty soon others got involved and it was like a party. It made me pretty nervous. I was tape-recording, but I would have to leave the room and go out to the car every once in a while because it was making me nervous. I figured that what was going on was really over the line.

It was too grim to be a spectator sport, that's for sure. I left my tape recorder running inside where the action was taking place, but I didn't stand there and watch it all the time. But I had to record it because that's the stuff you use when you write.

RON BEVIRT: Neal was really hurt by his friend's involvement in the gang bang. He was also high on acid. So after he took his turn, he went outside and kneeled down behind one of the Angels' bikes and began sucking. I looked out and there was Neal crying and sucking on this tailpipe. This was one of those perfect psychedelic statements.

HUNTER THOMPSON: It was weird peer pressure. Imagine the pressure that would cause you to drop your pants while the Hell's Angels fuck your friend? It was weird, no matter what you think.

RAM DASS: Everywhere you looked there were red lights flashing. The police never came on the grounds, but the minute anyone left the property, they searched the car. I remember I had a rental car for some reason and I had nothing in it. But they wrote me a ticket anyway because one door wasn't completely closed.

Kesey was never interested in protesting the Vietnam War the way everyone else was. In what was no doubt intended to be a mock-serious, ironic declaration, he told Lee Quarnstrom, "Why should I care about a little island in the Pacific?" In the same spirit, during the Vietnam Day protests,

he told a group of protestors: "There's only one thing to do, there's only one thing that's gonna do any good at all. And that's everybody just look at it, look at the war, and turn your backs and say, 'Fuck it.'" Still, Allen Ginsberg and several of the Pranksters met with Hell's Angels president Sonny Barger to try and convince him to keep the Angels from fighting with anti-war protesters who were blocking shipments of war materials from the Oakland Army Terminal. Despite sharing LSD with the Pranksters and discussing the issues at length, the Angels wouldn't budge from their belief that the anti-war protesters were Communists and couldn't be supported. According to Hunter Thompson, this marked the end of the period of peace and harmony between the Pranksters and the Angels.

HUNTER THOMPSON: In the beginning it was such a wonderful marriage that the honeymoon went on for two or three months. It was a massive consolidation that was good for me because I could do three stories at once. I was working on stories that dealt with Berkeley, Angels, and drugs, so I could pull them all together. But the alliance fell apart when Ginsberg tried to bring Kesey into the Berkeley situation. Kesey and Ginsberg were trying to get the Angels to calm down and become anti-war activists. Kesey, Ginsberg, and Lee Quarnstrom were trying to get the Angels to act as bodyguards for radicals in Berkeley who were fighting with the Oakland police. Kesey believed they would do it. Ginsberg believed they would do it. I said, "No, it's not going to work."

It was the second time I had said something with the Angels wasn't going to work, but this time I knew it wouldn't. I didn't even go to that march. But I remember that the Angels, along with the Oakland police, turned on the Berkeley leftists and attacked them. I think Kesey actually got stomped and whacked around at one point. Things with the Angels kind of went to hell after that.

There was a minority—but a hardcore minority—of Angels that really understood Kesey. They were all in the San Francisco group, which was really a different kind of group anyway. They were much more hippie-oriented, more into flower power.

This was the group I met first and I never had any trouble with them from the start. When I went up to see them the first time, I went out wearing wing-tipped shoes and a madras sports coat and tie. I ended up

POETS "MARETTA," ALLEN GINSBERG, AND MICHAEL MCCLURE AT THE "BE-IN" AT SAN FRANCISCO'S GOLDEN GATE PARK ON JANUARY 14, 1967, WHICH ALSO FEATURED THE GRATEFUL DEAD, QUICKSILVER MESSENGER SERVICE, JERRY RUBIN, LAWRENCE FERLINGHETTI, AND GARY SNYDER. (GENE ANTHONY)

inviting them to my apartment and we sat around the fire listening to Dylan. That was the San Francisco group.

When I got into writing the book [*Hell's Angels*], and went across the bridge, I had a whole new world open up in front of me. The Oakland group was pro-war—there were differences even between Angel chapters—so when all this stuff happened in Berkeley, it strained relations to the point where there was violence between the San Francisco and Oakland chapters.

At times the Pranksters appeared to side with anti-Vietnam War demonstrators, while at other times they seemed to side with conservatives, with such proclamations as "A Vote for Barry [Goldwater] is a Vote for Fun." Other times, they were clearly in their own camp—the Prankster camp—with occurrences like this one:

LEE QUARNSTROM DURING THE
LOS ANGELES ACID TEST PERIOD,
JUST BEFORE LEAVING FOR
MEXICO TO MEET UP WITH KESEY.
(RON BEVIRT)

THE ACID TEST GRADUATION. RAM DASS: "IN A WAY [THE ACID TESTS] WERE LIVING THEATER . . . THERE WERE ATTEMPTS TO ENGAGE PEOPLE IN THEIR SENSES TOTALLY SO AS TO MAKE IT A TRANSFORMATIONAL EXPERIENCE THROUGH OVERLOAD . . . YOU KEPT FEEDING IN MORE AND MORE SENSE AND SOUND AND ENERGY AND LIGHT AND SO ON . . . I THINK IT WAS REALLY AN ATTEMPT TO FIND A COLLECTIVE CONSCIOUSNESS, MYTHOLOGY, IN THE JUNGIAN SENSE." (TED STRESHINSKY)

KEN BABBS: I'll tell you a good prank that Cassady did when we were in an anti-Vietnam War rally in Berkeley, and it was just loaded with FBI agents and cops. They were all plainclothesmen, but they all had a button that they wore that identified them and, after a while, everybody knew who they were. So we were standing there and a bunch of protesters were screaming and yelling at the cops and these cops were screaming and yelling back and it was really going back and forth—"Heyaryoutherewhatyadoingyousonabitch!"—in these harsh voices. And Cassady walks by and he hears this hostility flying back and forth and he pulls a pack of gum out of his pocket and goes right up between them and says, "Hey! Who wants gum ayunahonah?!" in the same tone of voice. "I got gum here! Best gum in the world, really screw you up." And he was being the same way they were—loud, belligerent—but offering chewing gum. It just bewildered them—sent their minds skewering. It confused them so much that all the hostility petered away to nothing.

GOON KING BROS.
"DIMENSIONAL KREEMO"

RUDY KLOPTIC

My Name is LEE QUARNSTROM
I live at 3125 Soquel, Soquel, Calif
I was born 11/13/38
I am 6' 4" tall, have blue
eyes, blond hair, and weigh 155
I am a member of INTREPID
TRIPS, INC. and am doing nothing.
Lee Quarnstrom

My Name is RONALD K. BEVIRT
I live at THE BUS
I was born 20 OCT 1939
I am 6 FT tall, have GREEN
eyes, BROWN hair, and weigh 180
I am a member of INTREPID
TRIPS, INC. and am doing nothing.
Ronald Bevirt
Signature

HASSLER

✦ KEN BABBS ✦

Intrepid Trips, Inc.
345 Franklin Street. San Francisco. (415) 861-1151
(Can you pass the Acid Test?)

CAN
YOU
PASS THE
ACID TEST
?

PRANKSTER WALLET CARDS (CLOCKWISE FROM TOP LEFT):

BUSINESS CARD FOR WAVY GRAVY'S "GOON KING
BROS.," A SAN FRANCISCO PSYCHOTROPIC SUBSTANCE
DELIVERY SERVICE.

LEE QUARNSTROM'S PRANKSTER I.D. CARD WHICH
SAID, FOR THE BENEFIT OF THE POLICE, THAT THE
HOLDER WAS "DOING NOTHING."

"INTREPID TRIPS, INC.," BUSINESS CARD.

UNCLE SAM LOGO THAT APPEARS ON OBVERSE
OF PRANKSTER I.D. CARDS.

RON BEVIRT'S PRANKSTER I.D. CARD.

As Robert Stone put it: "Sometimes I feel like I went to a party in 1963 and it sort of spilled out the door and into the street and covered the world." The door they spilled out of was that of the Spread, which was Ken Babbs's hideaway near Santa Cruz. Today, this area is an expensive place to live; the Spread is probably condos. But back then it was a run-down farm with rusting vehicles, beat-up buildings, and Day-Glo paintings tacked to walls — to spruce the place up a bit. This was the site of the first Acid Test.

A number of new recruits came to the first Test, attracted by a sign hung in Ron Bevirt's Santa Cruz book store. The sign read: "Can YOU pass the Acid Test?"

Most of the outsiders left by 3 A.M., leaving the La Honda crowd to themselves, talking about a Kesey idea of Vietnam protest — turning your back on the war and walking away.

The second was in San Jose, the night of the Rolling Stones concert. Test number three was in Mountain View.

The fourth Test was at Muir Beach, north of San Francisco, and promised the vaudeville talents of Neal Cassady and Ann Murphy, and the music of the Grateful Dead. And there was to be a showing of the movie of the bus trip.

These were the northern California Acid Tests.

LEE QUARNSTROM: The first Acid Test was held at a place called "the Spread" — as in what a rancher would call his ranch. This was a little ranch in Soquel, which is a small, unincorporated town adjacent to Santa Cruz. I lived on the Spread with Babbs and Gretchen Fetchin and Ron Boise and Space Daisy, whom I later married after Boise died. They lived there in Boise's big truck. Kesey and Faye and their kids and Mountain Girl lived there on and off too.

It was about 400 acres, but we rented it pretty cheaply because Santa Cruz was not a hot place to live in those days. We had left La Honda for a lot of reasons, one of which was the septic tank had backed up and the Hell's Angels were hanging around too much. Many of us were not as enthralled by the Hell's Angels as others were.

Anyway, one night the first Acid Test just happened there at the Spread. It happened in the living room of the Spread. Allen Ginsberg was there, Cassady was there, Jerry Garcia and a couple of the Warlocks were there before they became known as the Grateful Dead.

NOTE FROM KEN KESEY—
"SWASHBUCKLER" TO PAGE
BROWNING—"DES PRADO"—
CONCERNING POLICE TROUBLES
PRANKSTER SANDY LEHMANN-
HAUPT HAD THE PREVIOUS
NIGHT. (RON BEVIRT)

It was like a Mickey Rooney movie where we suddenly said, "Hey, I know, we can put on a show."

ED MCCLANAHAN: The first time I remember anybody calling these things Acid Tests was at a party up at La Honda one night at which Kenneth Anger turned up. His trip, you know, is film noir and real esoterica and erotica. Kenneth Anger showed up for some obscure reason and then got mad and left when somebody decided to sacrifice a chicken. Everybody was amazed because they all thought that sacrificing a chicken was child's play to Kenneth Anger. But, as I recall, that was the first party that anyone referred to as an Acid Test.

LEE QUARNSTROM: The next Acid Test was at a black guy's house in San Jose who went by the name of "Big Nig." He lived in an old duplex near San Jose State University. The Grateful Dead played and everybody took acid. I remember Zonker coming up to me saying that the Red Chinese were attacking, which he believed. But other than that, it wasn't memorable.

During the period of the Acid Tests, police were virtually stationed along the side of the road near the Kesey house. Finally, in April 1965, Kesey and fourteen Pranksters were arrested there. Lee Quarnstrom recalls that most of the charges were marijuana possession and, additionally, Kesey was charged with operating a premises where marijuana was furnished, and with resisting arrest.

RON BEVIRT: When did Kesey first get cross-ways with the law? Well, at some point after the bus trip, there was a raid on La Honda. I mean, the cops had been noticing this scene going on at La Honda for some time. I think maybe even the neighbors complained about the noise because there was this loudspeaker stuff going on all the time. Heaven knows how anybody that lived within hearing distance of that tolerated it and didn't come over and start firing away.

Out on bail a few days later, Kesey's battles with the law began. He took a rap for Neal Cassady, whose previous conviction for possession of a single joint put him in jeopardy of mandatory jail time. After over a dozen court

appearances Kesey was given a suspended sentence, on the promise that he would no longer associate with the other Pranksters.

Meanwhile, in Berkeley, Denise Kaufmann was puzzling over the nature of her acid experience at the Greek Theatre.

APRIL 1965 ARREST OF FOURTEEN PRANKSTERS ON MARIJUANA POSSESSION AND RELATED CHARGES AT KESEY'S HOUSE IN LA HONDA. FLANKED BY SAN MATEO COUNTY DEPUTY SHERIFFS ARE (L. TO R.): KEN KESEY, LEE QUARNSTROM, AND NEAL CASSADY.

DENISE KAUFMANN: I couldn't talk to anybody about my experience because it was before anything was going on where people were talking about out-of-body experiences. Today it's different. But then I was very alone with this experience.

About two days later, I still looked really weird, a friend called and said that there was a conference down at Asilomar, a Unitarian Church conference center, and his dad wanted us all to come down there. So we

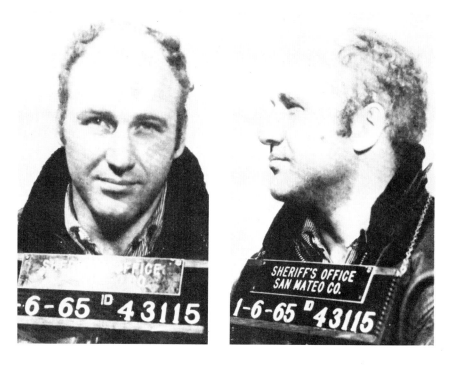

packed our electric guitars and some amps and stuff into my car and went to the conference. That was where I met Kesey.

LEE QUARNSTROM: Kesey had been invited to speak to Unitarians at Asillomar, in Pacific Grove on the Monterey Peninsula. We had all just been arrested, and they wanted to hear his side of the story.

DENISE KAUFMANN: I had never heard of Kesey, by the way. But when we got there, we drove out to this campground by the ocean and there was this bus painted all these colors. Everything was fluorescent. It was like the whole world had been in black and white and all of a sudden there was technicolor. We got there and there were all these people—the Pranksters—up on stage reading poetry about Jesus in hip talk. Someone was up there reading, and other Pranksters were walking through the audience with these long scarves, weaving them across people's faces and around their bodies. These Unitarians were not used to this; they looked like they were in shock.

LEE QUARNSTROM: Kesey spoke to the Unitarians and captivated them with his magic. Then he took everyone out to the sand dunes, and as the sun was setting he said, "Something magnificent is going to happen in a moment." And as the sun went down it hit the ocean just right and there was this incredible green flash, which is a natural phenomenon that happens when the atmospheric conditions are just right. But for Kesey to be tuned in to the fact that this was going to happen was impressive.

DENISE KAUFMANN: Afterwards we had coffee and cookies and milled around. Like I said, I didn't know who Kesey was. But while I'm drinking coffee, this guy comes up to me, looked at my broken face, and says, "What happened to you?" I said, "Oh, you wouldn't believe it if I told you." And he said, "Try me." So I told him about walking on air off the stage at the Greek Theatre. He didn't look shocked. "Meet me when this thing is over. We'll talk." So I met him afterwards and we went down to the beach and spent the whole night on the beach talking. Kesey was the first person I met who could give voice to the experience I'd had.

In the morning we walked over to the lodge and he took me into this room where his wife Faye was staying and pointed at me and said, "She knows." And I didn't know what I knew.

That afternoon we plugged in our instruments and played. Kesey was really blown away. He had never heard a reverb unit on a guitar before.

About a week later Kesey showed up at my apartment in Berkeley and said, "I've come to get you. Pack. Come and live with us at the farm." And I did it. A major life decision in one second. That's how I got involved in the Acid Tests. . . .

It was around this time that Kesey traded in his saxophone for an electric guitar, and started messing around with echo and reverb units. We were putting big speakers in the trees at La Honda and wiring them all together so that when you said something it would echo through all the trees. Roy Seburn and everybody were starting to get into light shows and all the stuff that we eventually used at the Acid Tests.

ED MCCLANAHAN: They were working on film all the time and other stuff, too. For instance, they were going to make a record of Neal. It was going to be 45 r.p.m., a single, and it was just going to be called "Drive."

They had these tapes that they had made of Neal talking while driving and they got a little band from up in the woods to come and do the back up music. I was there the night they did that. The group was named "Robin and the Hoods." Ken signed them up for this gig and under his direction they put together this piece of music that was to be background. I can't remember the tune exactly, but it would remind you of the "Batman" theme. It was perfect for Neal, very frenetic and fidgety.

What I remember about that session was that these guys weren't a terrific band by any means, and Ken was directing them as to how to do this piece of music. I mean, he can play the guitar a little bit and he definitely has some musical ability, but he is not in any sense a musician. Yet he would tell these guys, "Don't go 'do, do, de, de, du, du,' go 'pa, de, da, da.'" He knew what he wanted them to play and he made them play it. It was remarkable. It was kind of like directing people to build a building when you aren't an architect.

KEN BABBS: We tape-recorded Cassady and had ideas of getting out these records. But when we did it in '65 and '66, nobody could understand him.

It seemed like he talked so fast that you couldn't keep up with him. But now you listen to these tapes and they're totally comprehensible, it makes total sense, and even people that have never heard of him before laugh and think it's the funniest thing they ever heard, and it's not at all confusing. That's how much the world has changed in 25 years.

Silent use by artists, psychiatrists, and other interested parties kept LSD legal. But the Acid Tests brought it into general use and out in the open where the federal government could get a shot at it. As psychedelic society gained a profile, many of those who, like Ram Dass, were interested in "serious" research became concerned that regulation was right around the corner.

RAM DASS: I remember the first time that I saw, in the *San Jose Mercury*, a story about a "drug orgy." I realized at that point that Ken and

(OPPOSITE PAGE) GRATEFUL DEAD
MEMBERS JERRY GARCIA AND
PHIL LESH AT THE CORNER OF
HAIGHT AND ASHBURY STREETS
IN SAN FRANCISCO. (TED
STRESHINSKY)

the group were forcing the society to reckon with this stuff that we had hoped would stay underground a little longer. I felt that the Acid Tests forced drug legislation.

It was our whole hope that before society caught onto the heresy that was inherent in acid, we could get more entrenched into the policy-making levels. We were spending time meeting with psychiatrists and turning on people connected with the government—as well as major philosophers and poets—people who could be a voice for this stuff that undercut established social structures. Kesey brought it to the surface too fast.

LEE QUARNSTROM: Then there was another Acid Test in Mountain View. This one was bigger. It was held in a dance hall where the Grateful Dead could actually hook up electric instruments. I would guess that there were about 200 people at the one in Mountain View. I don't have any idea how they heard about it. Probably on the acid grapevine.

DENISE KAUFMANN: Mountain View was an amazing event. The Grateful Dead were fully set up and playing great stuff. That was when Pigpen was singing R&B songs like "Turn On Your Love Light." Pigpen's dad was the only white deejay on a black station and he was raised listening to R&B, so he sounded black.

At one point, I was standing out in the parking lot talking to Jerry Garcia, and this police car drove up and the officer got out and started questioning us. It was the usual: "What's going on here?" Jerry did most of the talking. Whatever Jerry said satisfied him because he turned to leave. As he turned to walk away, Jerry kind of tipped his hat and said, "The tips, captain."

The way he said it just knocked me out. I told Kesey about this interaction and out of that Jerry got his name, "Captain Trips."

RAM DASS: My general feeling is that the Acid Tests were extraordinary. I felt they were sheer magic. And they were scary magic. In many ways I saw it as religious ritual.

I call them scary because there were clearly bad trips going on within the framework of the Tests. They seemed to me to be not bad trips in the

sense that they were lethal, but bad in the sense that people were getting more than they bargained for.

Those of us from Millbrook saw acid tests as religious rituals and sacramental events. Going into the Acid Tests we still thought that acid had that quality about it that made us feel like religious seekers or research explorers. But the Acid Tests were different in that they had an incredibly strong sensual immediacy. They turned people inside out into the moment, in a way that they felt extremely alive. These events were crowded, wild, and confusing; they almost demanded surrender. For some, the surrender was great; but others didn't like that feeling of having no safe ground.

I remember watching someone, who thought he was coming to have a great pleasure, suddenly look at a wall and I could see that the wall was showing him things that were so profound it was shattering his reality, and I could see the look of horror in his face. I interceded; I talked to him and held him.

The Acid Tests were a rich source for the art that defines the sixties, the most notable being the Grateful Dead, who Timothy Leary calls "a twenty-year extension of the Acid Tests." Poster art sprang from the Acid Tests, too, as did the light show, a visual accompaniment to many rock shows that was designed to enhance the rock and roll experience—no matter what shape your neurons were in. The maestro, at this point, was Kesey himself.

ED MCCLANAHAN: I think Kesey found a new medium in the Acid Tests. Nowadays people call it "performance art." You know, those were the days when people were doing Happenings and Be-ins. I don't imagine Ken would like the association very much, but psycho-drama was going on. I think what he was doing with these groups was making art.

DENISE KAUFMANN: When we did the Muir Beach Acid Test, Wavy Gravy became a part of the scene. To me the two beings that kind of had the most direct access to some other arena of consciousness were Wavy and Neal.

KEN KESEY AND THE PRANKSTERS TAKE THE BUS THROUGH SAN FRANCISCO. ROBERT STONE: "RATHER THAN LAY DOWN AND LICK HIS WOUNDS WHEN HE WAS BEATEN BY THE SYSTEM, KEN DOUBLED HIS ANTE. HE DID THAT BECAUSE HE'S A WRESTLER; KEN ALWAYS THOUGHT LIKE A WRESTLER. HE WOULD LOOK AROUND AT THE SCENE AND LOOK FOR THE POINT OF LEVERAGE. IT WAS AS IF HE WAS GOING TO SOMEHOW GRAB THE SITUATION AND CHANGE THE *TAO*. HE WAS ALWAYS LOOKING AROUND TO TRY TO FIND THE CENTER OF BALANCE. WHEN THE WORLD LEANED ON HIM, HE JUST UPPED THE ANTE AND FOUGHT BACK." (*SAN FRANCISCO CHRONICLE*)

WAVY GRAVY: I ended up in San Francisco with a comedy group called The Committee.

Another member of that group and I started a psychotropic substance business called "Goon King Brothers Dimensional Kreemo," in which my code name was "Al Dente," which I got from the cooking directions on a pasta wrapper. We had these lovely calling cards copied from the logo for *The Psychedelic Experience*, a book that Richard Alpert and Ralph Metzner put out. With that business we supplied the North Beach scene.

I don't think we made a lot of money, but we kept the cab company in business. I guess our greatest accomplishment was that at one point we could call Veterans Cab in San Francisco and just blow a whistle into the receiver and hang up. A couple minutes later they would come and pick us up.

We would take acid every Monday because that was our day off. I was up to about 750 micrograms. I would go zooming around the Bay Area checking out this or that. It was then that I got into the Muir Beach scene and met Kesey.

LEE QUARNSTROM: Stewart Brand did a thing called the Trips Festival. It was three days long and only one day was the Acid Test. It was pretty astounding to come to this festival and see how many people were doing related psychedelic stuff. It would be like getting to the North Pole and seeing three or four groups of explorers coming from the other direction—and feeling good about it.

RAM DASS: In a way, Kesey was developing a new medium. It was almost like Gandhi's line "My life is my message." It was the way in which one lived one's life that became art. To be a writer was part of it. The other was the crossover of sense domain—the sound becoming thought and the thought becoming smell. There were attempts to engage people in their senses so totally as to make it a transformational experience through overload. It was an attempt to overload one dimension so much that it forced people into another dimension.

In many ways, it was an attempt to find a collective consciousness in the Jungian sense.

DENISE KAUFMANN: Neal was one of the original rappers. Neal took rap to a new level. I would ride shotgun next to him and he would have this little mike around his neck and he would be rapping. He was like a weaver or someone that could take the whole of what was going on and put it together.

It's like everything that was going on would be separate, but there would be something about his energy that would rise up in between all the cracks and would be everywhere. He was like the creator of everything, the unifying sound of what was going on.

Kesey's second bust came on the night of January 19, 1966, two nights before Stewart Brand's Trips Festival. He and Mountain Girl were sitting on top of Brand's apartment building, smoking dope and tossing pebbles at a house across the street, when a police cruiser appeared on the scene. Kesey and Mountain Girl saw the police enter the apartment building, but he says he didn't connect their presence with his activity. The result was a second arrest for possession of marijuana, an offense that carried an automatic three-year jail sentence.

RON BEVIRT: Someone who lived in one of the other buildings, whose windows overlooked the roofs, had called the police and complained about this pebble-tossing.

Kesey and Mountain Girl watched the cops pull up in front of the apartment and point up toward the roof. Somehow, they didn't put it together that the cops were coming for them because they held onto a small amount of weed.

When the cops came up, Kesey realized what was happening and tried to throw the grass over the edge. It was a wild scene. One cop was tussling with him and the other cop had his gun pointed. The cop who was fighting with Kesey kept yelling, "Shoot him, shoot him now."

Kesey finally managed to throw it over the edge of the roof, but then the cops picked it up off the ground later.

STEVE LAMBRECHT: I felt bonded to Kesey, but not so bonded that I was willing to get busted with him. I think he wanted to get busted so he could force himself to become a fugitive. Why? For the adventure. He knew that first bust was coming down in La Honda; we all did. A lot of the guys didn't mind if they got busted, but I did. When it became obvious to me that a bust was going to occur in La Honda, I went to Nicaragua because I knew that if I was in town I wouldn't be able to resist going over to Kesey's place.

So, when Kesey got busted in San Francisco the second time, I left twenty minutes before it happened because I knew a bust was coming down. A bunch of us did.

I think it was obvious that night that Kesey was trying to run himself into a bust. I'll tell you why. We had gone to dinner somewhere in San Francisco and Kesey was smoking dope on the cable cars. We went to see a movie, *Juliet of the Spirits*, and Kesey was smoking dope in the theater. All of a sudden we began to realize, "Wait a minute, man, this guy is not just getting high. Something else is happening."

It was obvious to us that the police weren't seeking Kesey out. I mean, here he is on the roof of an apartment, smoking dope, and throwing rocks at people in the street and at a house next door. Hey, come on, man. Are we talking about getting busted here or what?

Stewart Brand took over where the Pranksters left off. He organized the Trips Festival, a "simulated" acid trip using lights and music. The three night festival would be held at the Longshoremen's Hall in San Francisco and would feature Ken Kesey and the Merry Pranksters the second night. Kesey's much-publicized bust was a boon to promotion of the event. All told, the festival grossed $12,500 in three days. Out of it sprang the Fillmore Auditorium and the career of rock music impresario Bill Graham. There was talk of a promoter taking it to Madison Square Garden. Another thing sprang out of it, too: Kesey was found guilty of possession and released pending appeal. He decided to go on the lam to Mexico to avoid prison.

LEE QUARNSTROM: Kesey had been busted again for smoking pot, so he and Mountain Girl had gone underground because he was facing two felony drug counts. So, the day of the Acid Test he couldn't show up as himself because he was a fugitive. So he came wearing a sort of mylar-like space suit and helmet and sat up in the balcony somewhere with a microphone and loudspeaker so he could talk on the public address

system. His voice was there, but none of the reporters or cops could find his body. He did meet with some reporters, finally, and announced he was running for Governor of California. After that, he split for Mexico. . . .

In those days, two possession of marijuana convictions were serious business. He also felt—and I can't help but agree with him—that the legal system was going to make an example out of him. Here's a famous and best-selling author who's thumbing his nose at the drug laws and, by God, we're not going to let him get away with it.

So he split for Mexico. But first he tried to stage his suicide. He had his cousin Dale, who looks a lot like him, drive his truck up the coast highway north of San Francisco, way up near Mendicino. Kesey had written what appeared to be a suicide note, supposedly written as he rambled along this road.

KEN KESEY [THE SUICIDE NOTE]: *Ah, the Fort Bragg sign and that means the ocean and that means time to drop the acid (not that I really need it, mind you; I've courage enough without chemical assistance, it's just that I'm scared . . .)*

Driving along, checking the abyss at my left like I'm shopping for real estate prospects. Ocean, ocean, ocean. I'll beat you in the end. I'll go through with my heels at your hungry ribs.

I've lost the ocean again. Beautiful, I drive hundreds of miles looking for my particular cliff, get tripped behind acid. I can't find the ocean, end up slamming into a redwood just like I could have slammed into at home. Beautiful.

So I Ken Kesey, being of (ahem) sound mind and body do hereby leave the whole scene to Faye, corporation, cash, the works. And Babbs to run it.

PRANKSTER ROY
SEBERN. (RON BEVIRT)

(And it occurs to me here that nobody is going to buy this prank and now it occurs to me that I like that even better.) [Signed Ken Kesey]

ROBERT STONE: Rather than lay down and lick his wounds when he was beaten by the system, Ken doubled his ante. He did that because he's a wrestler; Ken always thought like a wrestler. He would look around at the scene and look for the point of leverage. It was as if he was going to somehow grab the situation and change the *tao*. He was always looking around to try to find the center of balance. When the world leaned on him, he upped the ante and fought back.

In a way he became a character in his own book. He became McMurphy. McMurphy sacrifices himself on behalf of his people to take on the world. Ken did that.

LEE QUARNSTROM: The deal was that Dale was supposed to park the truck by a cliff and leave [Ken's] shoes and some other stuff and this note and make it look like Kesey had jumped off a cliff and into the ocean. But what happened, as I understand it, was that the truck gave out and Dale had to have someone tow the truck over to the cliff. He blew it.

Meanwhile, every time the FBI would come around they'd say, "We're looking for Ken Kesey" and we would always say, "Well, as far as we know, he committed suicide up north." Meanwhile, you could ask just about anybody on the street in Santa Cruz and they would say, "Oh, he's in Manzanillo or Mazatlan." So everybody knew but the FBI.

But even without Kesey, the Acid Tests spread to Los Angeles.

RON BEVIRT: Kesey didn't attend any of the L.A. Acid Tests. What happened was that he and I rented a red Mustang convertible in San Jose and drove to Los Angeles. Then he went off to Mexico in a truck with Ron Boise.

The rest of us started acid-testing our way south. We rented a series of houses in L.A. and had five, maybe six, Acid Tests in Los Angeles. We did one at Paul Sawyer's Unitarian Church, we did one in a sound stage, we did one in a movie hall, we did one in a garage in Watts after the riots.

WAVY GRAVY: I returned to Los Angeles. I was financing my life selling marijuana to the stars—in decorator bags with moon soldiers and things inside like Cracker Jack surprises. I also put on a show at the Aviation Academy called "Lysergic A Go Go." It was a real pioneering effort.

I was living in a house with songwriter Tim Hardin and an actress. It was at that house that Babbs came to show the film from the bus trip.

After that my wife and I and Del Close moved out of that house and found a house on Lemon Grove Street off Western Avenue. It was one of those L.A./Spanish-style houses with lots of wood, stucco, and lemon trees.

This is where I did my first really well-publicized event. It was called the "Lord Buckley Memorial Sunset." We had access to Moonfire Mountain, which was owned by Louis Beach Marvin III, the Green Stamp heir, who appears in the movies *Monterey Pop* and *Woodstock* wearing a black cloak and black hat followed by sheep.

He let me use his mountain because I had helped him out with his promotion of vegetarianism.

We sent out these beautiful invitations with a map on how to get to the mountain, and a quote of Buckley's song "The Flower."

The point of this event was to go up on the mountain and watch the sunset. But the day before, it started raining and raining and raining. We had all of this pineapple chili on the stove and people kept calling saying, "What about the Sunset?" I didn't know what else to do except to tell people that we were going to sleep on it and see how the next day came up.

The next day came up Day-Glo for me. I got up and there were about forty people dressed in Day-Glo clothing in the kitchen cooking eggs and anything else they could find in the refrigerator. They were the Prankster entourage and they had arrived in force for what would become the L.A. Acid Tests.

Tiny Tim was living in the back room and he was very distraught at the arrival of this crowd. He told me that "Mr. Neal Cassady" came at three in the morning and wanted some grass. Tim couldn't figure it out. He said that Neal was standing on a whole lawn full of grass. When I told him Neal was looking for marijuana, Tim was just shocked.

LEE QUARNSTROM: Our ultimate goal was to get together with Kesey in Mazatlán. We even had a date when we were going to get together. We were all working at the Hip Pocket Book Store, in Santa Cruz, that was owned by Hassler and his partner, Peter Demma.

We loaded up the bus and headed to the next Acid Test, which turned out to be in Sepulveda, north of the San Fernando Valley. We did it at a Unitarian Church, where we had been invited by a minister named Paul Sawyer.

Paul Sawyer was one of those Unitarians who was captivated by Kesey's presence. So he invited us to come down to his church and hold an Acid Test.

(OPPOSITE PAGE) JERRY GARCIA, TOM WOLFE, AND UNIDENTIFIED THIRD PERSON AT THE CORNER OF HAIGHT AND ASHBURY STREETS IN SAN FRANCISCO. (TED STRESHINSKY)

(OPPOSITE PAGE, INSET) MANY PEOPLE FIRST HEARD ABOUT KEN KESEY AND THE MERRY PRANKSTERS THROUGH TOM WOLFE'S BEST-SELLING BOOK *THE ELECTRIC KOOL-AID ACID TEST*. JACKET COPY ON THE FIRST EDITION OF THE BOOK CREDITS KESEY AND THE PRANKSTERS WITH HAVING "ORIGINATED AND SPREAD MOST OF THE LIFESTYLES THAT NOW MAKE UP THE 'PSYCHEDELIC' OR 'HIPPY' WORLD," ADDING THAT "THEY EVEN SET OUT TO TURN ON THE WORLD THROUGH THE ACID TESTS." THIS WORK OF "NEW JOURNALISM," PRESENTING RECONSTRUCTIONS OF EVENTS WITH ENERGIZED, POETIC LANGUAGE AND PRECISE OBSERVATION, WAS FIRST PUBLISHED IN 1968 AND QUICKLY HIT BEST SELLER LISTS. THROUGH 1989 THE PAPERBACK HAS HAD 31 PRINTINGS. (BOOK JACKET DESIGN BY MILTON GLASER)

WAVY GRAVY: "TINY TIM WAS LIVING IN OUR BACK ROOM AND HE WAS VERY DISTRAUGHT AT THE ARRIVAL OF [THE PRANKSTERS]. HE SAID THAT 'MR. NEAL CASSADY' CAME AT THREE IN THE MORNING AND WANTED SOME GRASS. TIM COULDN'T FIGURE IT OUT.... HE SAID THAT NEAL WAS STANDING ON A WHOLE LAWN FULL OF GRASS. WHEN I TOLD HIM NEAL WAS LOOKING FOR MARIJUANA, TIM WAS JUST SHOCKED."
(RON BEVIRT)

WAVY GRAVY: Anyhow, the phone kept ringing and ringing and I finally cracked and called off the Sunset. Instead I told everyone to meet at the Unitarian Church where the Acid Test was going to be held.

About four that afternoon, I started getting antsy about having called off the Sunset. I decided that I should just go up there and see what was going to happen.

So four or five of us drove up to Topanga Canyon to Moonfire. It was still raining. We got out of this car and started walking up Mud Slick Road, past the big metal sign that said "Police Dog Training Course," which not too many people went by unless they knew better. We kept slogging through the rain until we got to the place where we were going to do the Sunset. The minute we arrived the rain stopped, the clouds parted, and the most beautiful sunset that anyone could ever imagine went down.

That has always been an inspiration to me throughout the years. If our name is on a poster saying we're going to be somewhere—be there flood, earthquake, monsoon, you name it—we'll be there to do the show....

We left the sunset and went to the Unitarian Church. This wasn't a normal church. It was a wooden geodesic dome, an unusual piece of architecture. I don't remember much from the Test itself. I remember that some of the pineapple chili left over from the Lord Buckley Sunset got burned, and when we tried to flush it down the toilet it plugged up the whole Unitarian sewer system.

LEE QUARNSTROM: I was pretty high, so I can't remember a whole lot about this particular place. But the church itself was like a theater in the round, with carpeted steps coming up from the perimeter. I spent most of my time sitting on those steps because I was so high. . . .

It was off Olympic Boulevard in Central Los Angeles. It was a magnificent old place with a second floor rotunda balcony like you would find in a capitol building. We stayed there and made preparations to go out and put on other Acid Tests.

At this time we were thinking of doing it commercially. I don't think anyone had the idea that we could make a lot of money, but we thought we could support ourselves, maybe make enough money at the gate to support ourselves for the next week.

WAVY GRAVY: Then they held two more Acid Tests in L.A. The major one, of course, was the Watts Test. I got credited with putting the acid in the Kool-Aid at Watts, but I didn't really do it.

LEE QUARNSTROM: It was right after the Watts riot. I had the sense that we were the first white people to be there since the riot.

We held the Acid Test in an old automotive repair garage that was empty. We got a couple of thirty-gallon garbage pails and mixed Kool-Aid. Owsley had a couple of glass ampules with pure LSD in them and he poured it into the Kool-Aid. We did some quick mathematics and figured that one Dixie cup full of Kool-Aid equalled fifty micrograms of acid. The standard dose, if you wanted to get high, was 300 mics. So we told everyone that six cups would equal a standard trip.

After a couple of cups, when I was as high as I had ever been, somebody recomputed and realized that each cup held 300 micrograms. I remember hearing that and realizing that I had just gulped down 2000 micrograms. The rest of the evening was as weird as you might expect.

WAVY GRAVY: The reality was that I spent the evening saying that the Kool-Aid on the right is for kids and the Kool-Aid on the left is the

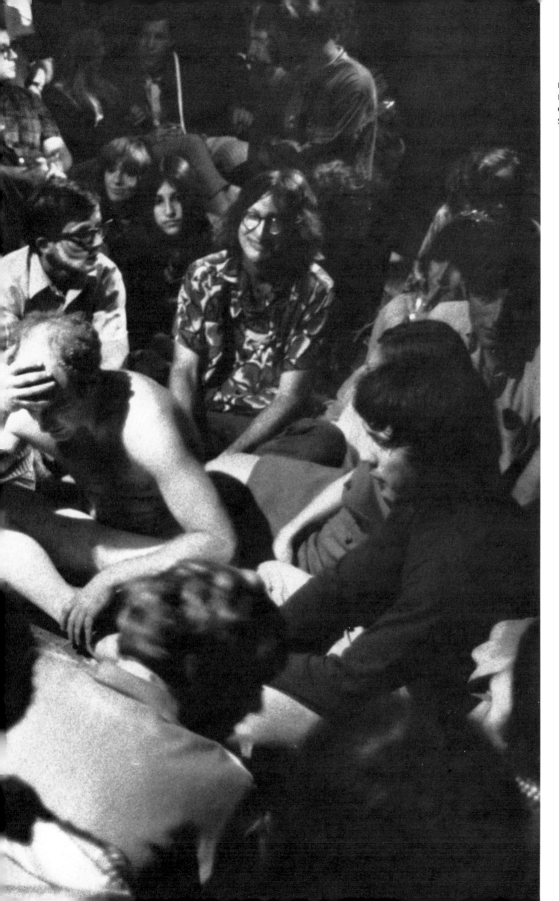

NEAL CASSADY AND KEN KESEY AT THE ACID TEST GRADUATION. (TED STRESHINSKY)

electric Kool-Aid. I just went on and on saying that the Kool-Aid on the right is for kids and the Kool-Aid on the left is the electric Kool-Aid.

People would be dancing for about three hours to the Grateful Dead and then they'd be looking for something wet. Well, "wet" was about 300 micrograms a swallow. That was pretty intense for some people, but if they wanted to go outside, there was nowhere to go because Watts was still smoldering from the riots.

DENISE KAUFMANN: It was really incredible. There were all these people with conga drums. It was like a whole primitive African conga scene, all these people on acid and the Grateful Dead playing. Owsley was freaked. He did not want to be a part of that scene. The Dead were freaked. Everyone was freaked.

RON BEVIRT: In the midst of this whole thing, I am showing my slides. I had these color slides of beautiful flowers and cacti, stuff like that. The Dead were playing and light shows were going on. But I'm sitting there, flicking my Kodak Carousel and changing these pictures, when three or four cops walk in shoulder to shoulder. They just walk right into the middle of my picture and stand there, taking in this whole scene.

LEE QUARNSTROM: That was also the night that the state narcs came in and just looked at people. They looked into our eyes with little flashlights to see what happened to the pupils. LSD was going to become illegal in the foreseeable future and they just wanted to see what LSD people looked like.

RON BEVIRT: And there was this one kid from Santa Cruz who was about six-foot four-inches tall. His name was Ox. And Ox walked up and put his face about two inches in front of these cops' faces and said, "I'm so high, I am so far out. Where I am, my consciousness is so far beyond anything that you can comprehend."

The cops never said a word. They just turned on their heels and walked out. "Way to go, Ox," I thought, "now they are going to come in and throw a net over us." But they didn't.

DENISE KAUFMANN: Outside they put up all of these wooden sawhorses. I mean the place was cordoned-off by wooden sawhorses and surrounded by the whole Watts riot squad with helmets and billy clubs. They weren't coming in, they were just waiting.

WAVY GRAVY: Somewhere in the middle of this, a young woman came unglued. She began screaming and screaming, "Ray! Ray! LSD! LSD! Who cares?! Who cares?!" It was being bombarded into everybody's DNA. "WHO CARES?! WHO CARES?!"

LEE QUARNSTROM: So following Babbs's law, which reads, *If you take a bad situation and irritate it, it will get worse,* he went over and stuck a microphone next to this woman's mouth. We had this kind of reverberation sound system. There would be an echo in one speaker that would come out another and so on. So we could hear this woman's "Who cares?!'" going on for a long time.

WAVY GRAVY: Well, I certainly cared, at least to get her to shut the fuck up. If she was unglued, I might at least find some way to get her glued back together. I went looking for her—twenty minutes, twenty years, who knows how long it took to find her—and found her standing in the middle of a circle of Pranksters and people I didn't know still saying, "Who cares?! Who cares?!" I got everybody to join hands which caused this woman to laugh and turn into jewels and light.

That was when I passed my Acid Test. I realized that when you get to the very bottom of the human soul and you're sinking, but you'll still reach for someone who is sinking worse than you are, everybody's going to get high. You don't need acid to get there.

LEE QUARNSTROM: Another thing I remember was Pigpen, the late singer with the Grateful Dead. He was a drinker and was afraid of drugs, but somehow he had gotten some acid and was now deep into a trip.

Someone had gone out and gotten some Kentucky Fried Chicken and he was trying to eat a drumstick. I say "trying" because he stood there for about fifteen minutes staring at this drumstick. He was absolutely frozen into a statue.

The Grateful Dead weren't exactly functioning, either. They kept tuning things up and trying to get things to work but they didn't play any actual music. They were just too high to function. . . .

Also, Paul Foster had painted his face half blue and half silver. When he left the garage, the police arrested him for public drunkeness or something of the sort. I bring that up because Jack Webb later used that in a "Dragnet" series. It was about a bunch of LSD addicts taking this drug and how one of the guys painted himself blue. They called him "blueboy" on the show.

DENISE KAUFMANN: After the L.A. Acid Tests I dropped out of the Pranksters. At the end of the Watts Test I was taking a lot of acid so when everybody was starting to come down in the morning, I was really going up. And while we were in the bus on the way to the Watts Towers, Neal kept pointing at me. He saw ectoplasm coming out of my mouth and he kept telling me that he wanted to do a seance with me and Gavin Arthur [a noted psychic and direct descendant of President Chester A. Arthur] in San Francisco. I declined.

Anyway, we got to the Watts Towers and climbed around. I was feeling pretty spread out at that point.

I ended up back at Wavy's house. I sat across from Wavy and we played this game where he would breathe out and I would catch the breath by breathing it in. We just sat there and played catch with this one breath for hours. It was a powerful experience.

LEE QUARNSTROM: There was at least one other Acid Test; that was held on Pico Boulevard in an old sound stage.

It was a pretty crowded one. We had driven down Sunset Boulevard handing out fliers that said, "Come to the Acid Test." We did an interesting thing at this test. We didn't put any acid in the Kool-Aid. We had the same garbage can full of Kool-Aid but there was no acid in it. We put in some dry ice so it bubbled, but nobody took any acid at all. Still people thought they were high and acted high. It was a psychedelic placebo effect.

TIMOTHY LEARY: I don't think that the Acid Tests made the federal government move any quicker toward a clamp down on acid. What the

Pranksters were doing was an authentic pagan religious ceremony that initiated thousands of people. By the way, I never heard of any casualties from it. There were 3000 people in one of those warehouses with electric Kool-Aid and I never heard of any casualty rate.

Out of those Acid Tests we have a living, growing flower known as the Grateful Dead. Several hundred thousand people go to see them each year. It is almost like the bus. They just keep travelling.

WAVY GRAVY: At this movie sound studio Acid Test they wanted everybody to pose for the cover of *Life* magazine. That was when Babbs stole the bus and left to join Kesey in Mexico. I don't know why he didn't want to be photographed. Maybe he thought doing that kind of thing was tacky.

TIMOTHY LEARY AT THE POLO FIELD AT GOLDEN GATE PARK DURING THE JANUARY 1967 "BE-IN." (GENE ANTHONY)

LEE QUARNSTROM: Because Kesey was down in Mexico Babbs was more or less trying to fill in for him. He was sort of the officer of the day. There was a strong yearning in the group to stop doing more of these Tests and get down to Mexico. Kesey was like an energizer—a battery—and I think a lot of us felt that we needed some Kesey input.

We also felt that there were too many people on the bus that didn't really fit in. Babbs decided who should get on, who he wanted around, and who he didn't. Babbs went around tapping the chosen ones on the shoulder, saying, "Get on the bus now." I was one of those that got on the bus. About a dozen of us finally went down to Mazatlán.

We were having a bad time at this point. There was a lot of dissatisfaction with Babbs assuming more power than the group was willing to give him.

And then there was the bus. It kept breaking down all the time. George Walker spent a lot of time under it, lying on his back, working on gears and motor stuff that was not running well.

During this time Hassler, Zonker, and I retreated to the back of the bus. We called ourselves "the back of the bus gang" and spent less time with Babbs and more time just by ourselves. In retrospect, I think we were just getting anxious to get somewhere and get off the bus and stop doing the Acid Tests and start having some fun again. The Acid Tests became like work after a while.

RON BEVIRT: Doing the Acid Tests had been hard work and everybody was ready for a vacation. In Mexico we weren't planning to work, we were just going to relax.

So we went to Manzanillo and started looking for a house to rent. And Hagen rented a car, without a license plate, from somebody for 300 pesos. That was OK, because we had picked up a license plate somewhere to cover a hole in the floorboards of the bus to keep the hot air from blowing on Neal's feet. It was a couple of years out of date, but in Mexico that didn't matter. We put the plate on the car to make it seem more legal.

STEVE LAMBRECHT: The car was a 1950 Ford. The license plate was an Arizona plate that was about 1960. And the registration was for a 1959 Volkswagen from New York. That is what we used to pass through checkpoints.

LEE QUARNSTROM: When we got to Mazatlán we checked into a hotel and contacted Kesey to meet us there. Meanwhile, Hassler had contracted some kind of infection and he had to have his prostate massaged. And in order to have his prostate massaged, somebody else had to do it—you can't massage your own prostate because of the way your finger bends or something.

So he was asking if anybody would massage his prostate, and I said, "God, no!" So finally, somebody who was always dependable in helping with whatever work had to be done said, "I'll do it." So then he said, "Does anybody have any rubber gloves?" Nobody had any rubber gloves, but somebody had a condom. So Hassler bent over, and we were all just sitting around smoking dope and having a good old time, and this guy had this condom on his finger and had it up Hassler's asshole. The door opened and Kesey walked in and said, "My God, it's come to this!"

ROBERT STONE: While Kesey was down in Mexico I got a note from him that said, "Everything is beginning again." I didn't know what it meant. But when I started telling my literary agent about it she said, "Can you write about it?" I said, "Well, it might be pretty strange, but I can give it a shot." She called up *Esquire* magazine and they paid my way down there to hang around. Thus commenced the Mexican adventures.

LEE QUARNSTROM: So we got to Mazatlán and met Kesey, who was acting real paranoid. He actually thought there were agents spying on him. He was a fugitive, but I don't think anybody in Mexico gave a shit.

Still, he spent a lot of time looking over his shoulder and saying, "Oh, there's somebody over there looking at me." I remember a 1953 Ford drove by and he said, "That car has gone by here three times." It was stuff like that.

ROBERT STONE: The Federales were definitely watching us. Babbs, Kesey, and I had this extremely weird conversation with this guy who called himself "Agent Number One." He introduced himself and showed off his badge which had "numero uno" imprinted on it. He told us he was checking into reports that there were Russian spies around. He took us down to this local shrimp restaurant and plied us with rum.

He himself got extremely drunk and when we tried to buy him a drink he got very pissed off because he thought we were trying to get him drunker.

Nobody knew what was going on with the Mexicans, only that there was a sense of tension and a lot of jokes about the Alamo.

Some time after Kesey hit the Mexican frontier, Babbs, Gretch, George Walker, and Ron Bevirt had followed. They found their compadre in

A CHARACTER CALLED "THE HERMIT," WHO AT ONE TIME LIVED NEAR THE CENTER OF PRANKSTER ACTIVITY IN LA HONDA. (TED STRESHINSKY)

THE BUS IN SAN FRANCISCO PROMOTING THE ACID TEST GRADUATION,
WITH STEWART BRAND RIDING ON THE BACK. (TED.STRESHINSKY)

Mazatlán. Mountain Girl was pregnant with a child fathered by Kesey. Accustomed to being foreigners in their own land, the Pranksters found being "strangers in a strange land" to be rougher going.

ROBERT STONE: Kesey was rather worried. He didn't know what the hell he was going to do next. I mean, he was a fugitive. I think he was having to deal with the Mexican authorities through a Mexican lawyer and I think this involved paying them off. People kept turning up who nobody knew. Things were a little out of control. . . .

It was a pretty bad scene. Everybody was very paranoid. We were all staying at a run-down old Purina feed factory outside of Manzanillo. Faye was down there with the kids. Gretch and Babbs were there, and Gretch was pregnant. And some very peculiar people showed up, some of whom later had some connection with the Manson family. Needless to say, there were some extremely bad vibes down there.

LEE QUARNSTROM: Kesey wanted to go to Mexico City. He wanted to talk to a lawyer he knew there regarding asylum as a political fugitive from the United States.

I had lived in Mexico City in 1960 and I had Mexican friends there and I knew my way around town, so I accompanied Mountain Girl and Kesey.

I'm pretty sure Faye wasn't with us by that time; I think she was in the States. Kesey was always kind of circumspect about his relationship with Mountain Girl. Everybody knew about it, but he didn't rub it in.

He was feeling very desperate at the time and still very paranoid. To illustrate: here was Mountain Girl, she was tall and she had dyed her black hair blonde, and I am tall and blonde and Kesey is blonde. So here we are walking down the streets of Mexico City and Kesey insists on staying twenty feet behind us, mixing into the crowd, trying in his own strange way to look like a Mexican.

We spent several days in Mexico City just having fun, mostly. By then the Pranksters had moved to Manzanillo so we took the train down there.

RON BEVIRT: Some of the stuff that happened was funny. Neal, for instance, was into spending hours throwing this hammer up into the air and catching it. He could catch it behind his back, and throw it and catch it with his other hand. It was his nervous amusement to do this for hours.

Anyway, one day Neal was out walking on the beach and he saw an old man out dancing around with this stick. The two got to talking and the old man asked Neal if he would like to have a stick fight. It seemed like a good idea to Neal, especially since he was in good shape from playing with his hammer. To cut the story short, the old man beat the shit out of Neal.

ROBERT STONE: Cassady was doing speed so he never ate and he never slept and he never shut up. He was bad news in Mexico. And, of course, he was paranoid. He had this hammer that he carried in a holster and he also had a parrot. Because Cassady never shut up, the parrot never shut up either. So when you walked into a room at the "Casa Purina" there'd be this voice, "Last time I was in Denver, man," and you turn around expecting to see Neal and see this parrot instead.

LEE QUARNSTROM: Here we were in Manzanillo when it comes time for Mountain Girl to have her baby. They decided that they wanted the baby to be a Mexican citizen because under American law it can remain a Mexican citizen until it is eighteen and then it has to choose whether it is going to be an American or a Mexican citizen. As a Mexican citizen, the parents can buy property in the baby's name without having to take in Mexican partners.

So to do this, Mountain Girl has to be married so there can be a legal father. She can't marry Kesey, because he's already married. So George Walker agreed to marry her. Only he didn't go to city hall with Mountain Girl and the rest of the Pranksters; George had to go pick up money that our lawyer had wired from San Francisco. So George Walker was at the telegraph office getting money while he was being married simultaneously at city hall.

ROBERT STONE: The Mexicans were very frightened of us; they thought we were very weird druggies. Mexican police were nosing around all the time. There was a community of American expatriates, a lot of whom were pretty sinister, and the Mexicans watched that whole group as closely as they could.

The Mexican attitude toward marijuana in those days was that it was low-class, something ruffians did. As a result, they just thought we were a pack of thugs.

After less than two weeks, several of the Pranksters were involved in a serious automobile accident. As Zonker points out, "Fun was getting hard to come by."

Having had enough of Mexico, Zonker, Hassler, and Lee Quarnstrom decided to go home. Kesey and the rest stayed behind.

LEE QUARNSTROM: Finally I left Mexico with Hassler and Zonker. We took the bus back to the border. At the border we ate about thirty Dexedrine tablets because we didn't want to carry them back over the border and, of course, we didn't want to throw them out. At that point I left the Prankster fold, and struck out on my own.

STEVE LAMBRECHT: We took a bus up to Tijuana. Between Lee, and Ron and I, we had 36 cents and a bottle of Dexamils. It was midnight on a Saturday and we hadn't eaten for a day.

We figured that we had to get to San Francisco. We split the Dexamils three ways. There were 32 of them, but since I was deemed the most sensitive to speed I took ten and they each took eleven. We started hitchhiking from there.

ROBERT STONE: I finally had enough, too. I drove with Babbs and Gretch and their kids and crossed the border back into Nogales, Arizona. Kesey went another route. We all got together again in Palo Alto.

ED MCCLANAHAN: How did Kesey get out of Mexico? I remember him showing me a driver's license that he had down there with the name "Jim Anglund" on it. The story that he told me was that he commandeered an old horse and rode it up to the border with an old guitar around his neck. He announced to the border guards that he was "Singing Jimmy Anglund," and that he had been over the border performing, and had been beaten up and had lost his identification and that was all he had left. He persuaded them to let him cross.

STEVE LAMBRECHT: We got a ride with a sailor. He taught us how to open beer bottles with the seatbelt buckle. Finally, we ended up with some third-rate rock-and-roll band singer's sister on Sunset Boulevard at eight on Sunday morning, having breakfast. We were still flying on speed. I think it was two more days before we all went to sleep.

We split up in Los Angeles. But we all hooked up again with Kesey at the "Whatever It Is" Festival at San Francisco State.

Kesey had been in Mexico eight months and was now ready to make his presence known in San Francisco. He began to make surprise public appearances in the Bay Area—a bold action considering his fugitive status—including one at the "Whatever It Is" Festival put on by Stewart Brand.

ED MCCLANAHAN: Whatever It Is was kind of a bullshit occasion, to tell you the truth. They smashed an old car with hammers and that kind of stuff. There was some kind of athletic event with a big weather balloon. The bus was there in a very public way, and Ken was walking around in a pork pie hat and his old beat-up sports coat, carrying a tape recorder and pretending to be collecting bird calls. Here he was, a wanted man, yet this was his disguise.

I spent a long time wandering around with him on the San Francisco State campus. He was amazingly cool, especially considering that the police were looking for him everywhere. You know Ken though, he knows no fear.

The Grateful Dead played that night in some ballroom and there was a campus radio station that the Pranksters had rigged up so Kesey could broadcast to the assembled multitudes; but that wasn't going to happen until very, very late.

WAVY GRAVY: I don't remember much about Whatever It Is. We ran into Owsley at the airport. He had a hollow shark's tooth filled with some stuff that he dropped on my tongue. I remember feeling extremely glint. Neal and I used to share a microphone, which is what we did this night at Whatever It Is. He threw a word at me and I threw a word at him. We'd create sentences and paragraphs and who knew where they were coming from.

That was one thing about Neal, he was always about three minutes ahead of everyone else. I don't know if he was a genius, because as Thelonious Monk says, "Everybody is a genius at being themselves." But I have found that the road of life is filled with people smoking at the ears to be like Neal. Little do they realize that it was hard enough for Neal to be Neal.

STEVE LAMBRECHT: I was in charge of music for Whatever It Is. That was my intro into the music business, and I decided real fast that I didn't want to do that. Bill Graham agreed to loan us the Jefferson

Airplane and the Paul Butterfield Blues Band after midnight. So we got them, free, and there was going to be an enormous jam session that was going to last all night long. It would have been really hot, but it freaked out the police so they closed it down. And that was the last major Acid Test.

ED MCCLANAHAN: A few days later Kesey came to my house in Palo Alto and stayed. He was there in the house for a week, living in a little old room down in the cellar. I was getting more nervous each day, yet at the same time it was fun. I was right down the street from the police station; I was in the 900 block and the police station was in the 700 block.

Meanwhile, there is Kesey on the Bay Area's "Most Wanted List." Herb Caen mentioned in his column that he had been seen, and there was more talk about him being right there in Palo Alto.

LEE QUARNSTROM: The police were seriously looking for Kesey. But when the FBI came to the Spread looking for him, Babbs and Gretch were there wearing matching space suits and sewing weird clothes. Babbs answers the door and the guy says, "I'm Agent Powell from the FBI." And Babbs notices that the guy is wearing a fraternity ring from the same frat Babbs belonged to in college. So the guy puts out his hand to shake and Babbs gives him the secret fraternity handshake. And Babbs says, "Hey brother, come on in!" Before the guy could get away, Babbs threw his arm around his shoulder and took him on a tour through the house—"Here's our sewing machine, and here's Gretchen Fetchin the Slime Queen, and here's where I painted the floor. . ."

One of the places Kesey showed up at was at Denise Kaufmann's bedside in a San Francisco psychiatric hospital, where she had been committed by her parents.

DENISE KAUFMANN: My friend and I were living in Palo Alto, and Wavy came down, and we took an acid trip. There was something about taking a trip with Wavy. We would go into another realm of consciousness and just stay there for days. Being around Wavy was always a jumping-off point for something else. And so, this particular time we had taken this acid trip, and after a day and a half, Wavy had to go back to L.A. to finish making a movie. At the end of that period, I guess, I was just . . . I don't know. Whatever I was, my parents committed me. I was in the middle of an acid trip when I went to their house and tried to communicate with them. It scared them.

They committed me to Mt. Zion Hospital in San Francisco, to the psychiatric ward. The doctors came in and told me that they couldn't legally keep me after 48 hours, but that my parents were so upset they would probably go to court and have me committed to someplace like Napa if I left. Since this place was better than Napa, I decided to stay.

While I was there, Kesey came back from Mexico. When he heard where I was he stormed the ward and said, "OK, we're sending the Hell's Angels and we're going to bust you out of here." I could see the headlines: "HELL'S ANGELS BUST INTO MT. ZION HOSPITAL." Kesey was sure it was like *Cuckoo's Nest*, and they had me, and I had been tamed or something.

But the truth of it was that while I was in the hospital I had met Ambrose Hollingsworth, who was the manager of Quicksilver Messenger Service. He had been paralyzed in a car accident, but we started writing songs together.

By then I had this drum kit in my room and had other musicians coming in to jam with me. While I was in the hospital I put together my band, Ace of Cups. So things were totally moving right on track for me. It just looked a little weird to Kesey.

ED MCCLANAHAN: After a week Ken said he was probably going to leave and go back to San Francisco. I can tell you the exact day because it was my birthday—October 5th—and I was teaching creative writing at Stanford then.

As I was leaving for class that day, Ken said that he might drop in on me that day. I said, "Don't tell me, don't tell me." But I didn't tell him not to come. I just wanted the deniability factor built in.

So I went over to the classroom in the English department, which was right over Mr. Stegner's office. The classroom had a frosted glass door. I was in the middle of my class when I saw this shadow with a pork pie hat approaching the door. And in he came. "I just came to wish you a happy

A COPY OF LEE QUANSTROM'S [*SIC*] ACID TEST DIPLOMA, WHICH WAS AMONG THOSE AWARDED AT THE ACID TEST GRADUATION IN SAN FRANCISCO. THEY WERE DESIGNED BY ILLUSTRATOR AND INVETERATE PRANKSTER PUNSTER PAUL FOSTER. (LEE QUARNSTROM)

birthday," he said. So I brought him on in and sat him down. Of course, all these students were reasonably hip and knew about all the stuff that had gone on. We talked for about the next twenty minutes. Five minutes before class was to be over I told him, "Look, I think that it would probably be a good idea for you to leave the room now, before the bell rings." He said good-bye and stole away—which is to say, he stomped out—and the class and I sat there for another five minutes until the bell rang. Then I gathered my stuff up, and went downstairs to my office and walked in. The secretary of the writing program was there, and she said, "Somebody just called here and said that Ken Kesey has been seen on campus."

There were still lame rumors circulating that he had jumped off the cliff and committed suicide. So the next day in the Palo Alto paper the headline read: "Kesey the Corpse Seen in Stanford Class."

RON BEVIRT: Before he left for Mexico, Kesey had done some videotapes that taunted the FBI. These had played on the news stations, so the Feds were really out looking for him.

One afternoon we were going down the freeway in this old truck of mine, when suddenly there was this station wagon next to us, filled with FBI agents, holding their badges out the window, and waving for us to pull over.

We went on a ways trying to figure out how to ditch them. We tried to take evasive action, but they were ready and followed us no matter what we did.

Finally we pulled over, and Kesey climbed the cyclone fence alongside the freeway and took off running.

The agents were off duty so they had turned in their guns for the day, but they did the best they could without them. One of the agents went after Kesey. Another one had me sit on the ground while he stood over me with a road flare.

Kesey found himself running across a playground. He said later that the playground made him think about his own kids—so he stopped running and turned himself in.

Kesey was charged with three felonies: possession of marijuana, from his first arrest in La Honda; possession of marijuana, from his second arrest in San Francisco; and a federal charge of unlawful flight to avoid prosecution. Kesey could have potentially served twelve years in prison, but the eventual sentence was relatively light.

A jury trial for the bust on Stewart Brand's rooftop ended in a hung jury. A second trial, five months later, ended in another hung jury. Rather than risk a conviction in the third trial, Kesey accepted the State's offer to let him plead "no contest" to a lesser charge of "knowingly being in a place where marijuana was kept." For that he got a ninety-day sentence.

One month later he lost his appeal for the La Honda bust, which carried a six-month sentence on a county work farm, a $1,500 fine, and three years probation—a punishment remarkably similar to the one that Randle McMurphy went to a mental hospital to avoid in *One Flew Over the Cuckoo's Nest*.

He was allowed to serve the two sentences concurrently at the San Mateo County work farm, just a few miles from La Honda.

After his release, Ken Kesey went back home to Oregon.

THE BUS'S DESTINATION SIGN, IN ONE OF ITS MANY INCARNATIONS. (RON BEVIRT)

AFTERMATH

That was then and this is now . . . 1990 . . . 25 years after the acid trips that launched a million heads. Where are the Pranksters now? What has become of Kesey and the thirteen original Pranksters who made the inaugural bus ride?

KEN KESEY ("Swashbuckler" or "The Chief")—raises cattle on his seventy-acre farm near Eugene, Oregon. He is a grandfather now. In 1988, while teaching a graduate writing course at the University of Oregon, he led his class in writing a group novel that was published last year with the title *Caverns*, under the name U.O. Levon. Levon is "novel" spelled backwards, and U.O. stands for the University of Oregon.

Kesey is still writing. He has published two collected works since *Sometimes a Great Notion*. The first book, *Kesey's Garage Sale*, is a collection of commentaries, plays, and drawings, and features an interview with Kesey by Paul Krassner. The second book, *Demon Box*, is a collection of longer essays, fiction, and semi-journalistic works that he wrote for *Esquire, Rolling Stone, Running* magazine and *Spit in the Ocean* (a literary journal produced by Messrs. Babbs and Kesey). He continues to give readings and will soon have two additional works in print—a fictional screenplay featuring Neal Cassady, that was written in 1978, and a children's book.

He has also been working on a novel about a Vietnam veteran set in a fictitious Alaskan town. It has been over 25 years since *Sometimes a Great Notion* was published, and this literary silence naturally raises questions about what has accounted for the delay between that novel and this one.

I had the pleasure of spending a month in China with Kesey in 1981, on assignment for *Running* magazine. We were waiting for an airplane at the Xian airport with our Chinese guide, who was a literature student at the University of Beijing. His access to American literature was limited to works written before 1960, so he was not aware of the literary reputation attached to the name Ken Kesey. Innocently, he asked Kesey a very pertinent question: "Mr. Kesey, why is it that so many American writers commit suicide?"

Kesey looked up, then pointed at the acoustical ceiling tiles overhead in the airport terminal, and said:

> The writer writes a great book and the praise from the critics takes them right to the ceiling. Then, with their second book, they try to lift themselves up through those little black holes and go even higher. They can't, but they just keep trying, bashing

KEN KESEY AT HIS FARM IN PLEASANT HILL, OREGON, 1984. (ANN CHARTERS)

their heads against the ceiling until they can't take it anymore, and they kill themselves or drink themselves to death. I've decided not to do that. I've just decided to come down from the ceiling a little and wait for one of those holes to open up for me to pass through.

One just might.

KEN BABBS ("The Intrepid Traveller")—lives on a ten-acre spread in Dexter, Oregon, where he writes and farms. With a grant from the Grateful Dead, he has been able to catalogue much of the film and audio-tape from the bus trip. He takes the material on the road and shows the bus footage to old and new fans.

MIKE HAGEN ("Mal Function")—runs a small real estate empire in Oregon.

GEORGE WALKER ("Hardly Visible")—has a farm and is part of a race car driving team working its way up to Indy cars.

JOHN BABBS ("Sometimes Missing")—is a free-lance writer in Eugene.

CHUCK KESEY ("Brother Charlie")—is an acidophilus yogurt magnate, producing the West Coast's "Nancy's Yogurt."

DALE KESEY ("Highly Charged")—is living in Oregon.

PAULA SUNDSTEN ("Gretchen Fetchin")—now lives in Portland, where she is converting an old grange hall into a theater.

RON BEVIRT ("Hassler")—lives near Santa Cruz, where he is self-employed as a general contractor.

STEVE LAMBRECHT ("Zonker")—returned to San Jose, where he owns and operates a hazardous waste disposal business.

JANE BURTON ("Generally Famished")—is a lawyer, "landlord/tenant—on the tenant side," and lives in East Palo Alto with her two children, one of whom she was pregnant with during the first bus trip, which explains the origin of her Prankster nickname.

SANDY LEHMANN-HAUPT ("Dis-mount")—lives in New York and has been involved in the recording industry.

KATHY CASANO ("Stark Naked")—lives in the San Francisco Bay Area and is an actress.

NEIL CASSADY ("Sir Speed Limit")—died in Mexico in February 1968.

AFTERMATH — A FAREWELL TO NEAL CASSADY

NEAL CASSADY. (RON BEVIRT)

Neal Cassady died in 1968, a year or so after the last Acid Tests, next to the railroad tracks that run through the town of San Miguel de Allende, Mexico. Because the way he died was symbolic of the way he lived — expending enormous energy, pushing his own capacities to their limits — the circumstances of his death have taken on mythic significance.

Writer Steve Dossey went to San Miguel de Allende to interview people who knew Neal Cassady and to unravel the mystery of his death. He has compiled the following account, which, he believes, is as close to the truth as anyone is likely to get.

STEVE DOSSEY:

Neal Cassady's Last Days

In late January 1968, Neal calls [his wife] Carolyn long distance, from the Mexican border. He continues to repeat the refrain, "I'm coming home." She advises him to go to Mexico, fearing that traffic violations will land him back in San Quentin. It's the last time they talk.

Neal has trouble crossing the border but is eventually whisked across disguised as a member of a film crew. The tourist visa is dated January 30, 1968. Neal gets off the train in San Miguel but his luggage is mistakenly dropped off at Celaya, approximately forty minutes away. He follows the dirt road into San Miguel and along the way notices a black beetle stuck in the spines of a prickly pear cactus. He enters the plaza, stares at the baroque spires of the cathedral, then locates the red-tiled colonial dwelling where [a companion] JB waits.

On February 3, Neal and JB quarrel. Neal leaves in an eruption of cosmic dust. His neck is as hot as the engine block of an Olds 88. The sun ducks below the hills. He heads for the depot to catch a train to retrieve his bags. Neal walks along the cobblestones of town that melt into the dusty trail divided by shaggy palms. The air swirls with the smell of burro urine and flies cling to the porch of a small store covered with Coke signs where he stops for a bottle of *cerveza*.

San Miguel is at an elevation of 7,000 feet and the evening air is becoming very cool. Adjacent to the train station is an old adobe church topped with three crosses. A wedding fiesta is underway, the train is never on time, so Neal joins the festivities. He drinks *pulque* and tequila with the dark men in cream colored pants. It's getting late, the train hasn't passed through, and he is short of cash anyway. He says "fuck it" and decides to walk the tracks to Celaya.

A quarter-mile or so down the rails and he feels terribly tired and hunkers in the brush to sleep. The combination of the cold, the depression, the alcohol, and the unending weariness are too much. Neal does not regain consciousness. His body is found by campesinos, loaded onto the back of a truck, and taken to the home of an old friend, Pierre Delattre, whose address was found in Neal's wallet, scribbled on a scrap of paper.

The body is taken to a small hospital in town. A witness recalled that Neal's face resembled a Mayan deity, carved in stone. No autopsy is performed. The body is taken to Mexico City and cremated. The death certificate indicates "general congestion" as the cause of death.

After an unendurable wait, Carolyn finally receives Neal's ashes from a very spaced-out JB. No one knows the exact circumstance of Neal's death nor his final words or thoughts. And perhaps it's best that way. We are left with memories, novels, and the mythology of a man who once said, "You can work yourself into anything but how do you get out of it?. . ."

Neal Cassady, remembered:

WILLIAM S. BURROUGHS:

Two Things I Remember

Two things I remember about Neal were his uncanny identification with cars and his capacity for silence. On one occasion we drove from Texas to New York in a moribund Jeep. Often we would drive for six hours without a word exchanged. Yet all this time he was keenly aware of his surroundings and could repeat from memory the signs we had passed. The Jeep was in such a condition of disrepair that only Neal could drive it. But I never had a moment's trepidation so long as he was at the wheel. He was a natural driver, in tune with every atom of the car which became an extension of himself. He was also one of the most relaxed and easy people to be with I have ever known, owing to an innate self-sufficiency.

COPY OF NEAL CASSADY'S
MEXICAN DEATH CERTIFICATE.
(STEVE DOSSEY)

RAILROAD STATION IN SAN
MIGUEL DE ALLENDE, MEXICO,
NEAR THE TRACKS WHERE NEAL
CASSADY DIED. (STEVE DOSSEY)

L A W R E N C E   F E R L I N G H E T T I :

Telegram on Cassady

LOOKING AT CASSADY PICTURES I SEE NEAL NEVER
STOPPED RUNNING NEVER SLOWED DOWN HE MUST
HAVE BEEN RUNNING DOWN THAT RAILROAD TRACK
IN SAN MIGUEL DE ALLENDE WHEN HE RAN OUT OF
TRACK AND SO NOW NEVER HAVE TO GROW OLD BUT
ALWAYS LOOK LIKE PAUL NEWMAN IN 'THE HUSTLER'
THE LOST COWBOY ON THE LOST RANGE TURNED INTO
A FREEWAY HIS HORSES WERE CARS AND HE NEVER
STOPPED RIDING AT STOPLIGHTS AND SLOWED DOWN
ONLY FOR LOVERS TALKING NONSTOP IN THE NIGHT
I HEAR HIS WHIZZER MONOLOGUE SEE HIM STREAKING
STILL HUSTLING OVER THE HILL A FLASH UPON THE
BRAINPAN HE'LL ALWAYS BE YOUNG & LOUD IN OUR
OLD HEARTS

6/79

LEE QUARNSTROM: Neal was an incredibly brilliant man. I read revisionist histories about the era that ascribe his astounding intellectual feats—like the ability to connect ten different things to one pun—to the use of speed. But in fact I think speed was not the engine that drove his intellect. It was his mind that was the astounding thing. Speed was just keeping him awake.

ROBERT STONE: Neal was a lot like that character Brando did in *The Wild One*, the real forties hipster. I remember he did things like taking a cigarette out without taking the pack out of his pocket. That was real jail cell behavior. I remember guys doing that on ships so they wouldn't have to pass a cigarette to everybody. He was a guy who had obviously seen the underside of America.

GORDON LISH: Kesey summed up Neal best when he spoke of him as Superman. That's what he was. In every consideration of the construction of a human enterprise that I can remark, I would regard Neal Cassady as some fantastic extreme. He was not an intellectual by any means, but he was certainly intelligent in nothing less than a miraculous way. But the quality about Neal that probably made him such a precious friend is that he had simply the dearest heart I've ever encountered in any human being.

RAILROAD TRACKS OUTSIDE SAN MIGUEL DE ALLENDE. (STEVE DOSSEY)

Editors' Epilogue

One of the stories that we weren't able to include earlier in the book we'd like to run here. Hunter S. Thompson recalls:

One of the wildest, heaviest, and best acid trips of my life happened during this period [of Acid Tests] at Richard Alpert's house in Palo Alto. I went crazy. I knocked out all the windows thinking I needed to do that to get air—that kind of thing.

I went back home to San Francisco, and saw the blood on my hands and realized what had happened, and thought, "Oh, shit, he had invited me down there, what did I do?"

So two or three days later I went back down there to make amends, offer some money to pay for the damages.

I got on the freeway and I was still as high as twelve kites.

Instead of heading to Alpert's place, I got off at San Bruno. I had locked onto the sunburst taillights of a Ford Mercury and got hypnotized. I locked onto those taillights like a cruise missile or something, and followed four feet behind them. My focus had shifted to the light. I was having a wonderful time. I was right there. I drove fine, perfect. I was like a freight car hooked up to a locomotive. I was right behind him.

I'd been following him from the freeway all the way to his house in the hills in San Bruno. I pulled into this driveway right behind him.

It was a family. I remember that people suddenly got out, terrified. The father was yelling, "What the fuck! You bastard, what do you want?"

I woke up, and I said, "Jesus Christ!" I just backed out and sped away.

What do we make of a story like this in 1990? In the 1960s it might have been easier to find an exhilarating, hilarious innocence in it. But we now live in a time when drugs and people who use them are considered to be, and can be, threatening. As Paul Krassner puts it: "There's a hysteria in the land now, and the whole culture's changed since the 1960s. Then, a stranger on the street could hand you a pill and you might try it because you liked the color of his halo, and now, of course, there's the Tylenol killer."

A central presence in this book is that of LSD. The innocence with which it is regarded may seem anomalous to the contemporary reader. However, the use of certain drugs in the 1960s occurred in a somewhat different context from that of drug use in the 1990s. For some people, as Paul Krassner says, "Acid served as a catalyst for expanding consciousness—and a lot of the drugs today are [purely] an escape from horrible realities."

There is another way in which our times may differ from the 1960s, which Robert Stone pointed out during one of the interviews for this book:

I was never very sentimental about the sixties except to the extent that they were the time of my youth. . . . I think that the United States became a freer country, partly as a result [of these times]. I think that the results, like all results of eras of transition, are indirect, but it was a time of tremendous hope and some of that hope was realized.

We have intended this book as a celebration of an era worth remembering, preserving, and keeping alive—an era of freedom, a time in recent history full with possibility. A time when a group of innocents, rejecting the blandness of the Eisenhower Era, would foreshadow the emergence of a vital, alternative culture with a simple cross-country bus trip.

In 1975, at a gathering in New York City, Ken Kesey offered a parable explaining how he regarded his role as a member of a counterculture:

About 400 years ago, Baal Shem-Tov, the founder of Jewish Hasidism, came to the King and said, "King, the wheat is all poisoned, and everybody that eats it this next year is going to go crazy."

The King says, "That's terrible. . . ."

And [Baal Shem-Tov] says, "I thought you would say that, so I thought we'd give each other the chance to put a little *x* on each other's foreheads, so that when we see each other later on we'll know that we *chose* to go crazy, whereas everybody else is just crazy."

A subtle distinction that makes an enormous difference.

—Neil Ortenberg
Michael Schwartz

THE BUS IN KESEY'S BARN IN PLEASANT HILL, OREGON, IN 1984. (ANN CHARTERS)

A Final Word

And what about the bus? That 1939 International Harvester school bus that got its immortality as the chariot to Ken Kesey and the Merry Band of Pranksters? That psychedelicized behemoth that somehow got a crew of fourteen across the country and back again? The Smithsonian Institution in Washington, D.C., has wanted Kesey to donate it to them for some time, and, as of this writing, there is a good possibility of this happening, as a backer has offered to finance the move. What has happened to the bus over the last 25 years?

After it travelled to Woodstock, in 1969, Kesey decided to retire it to his field in Oregon.

About ten years ago Kesey built an enormous block barn to house the bus and serve as an occasional writing studio. Kesey's hay needed a place to remain dry, so the bus got pushed out into a nearby field. It remains there today, having endured years of persistent Oregon rains.

—*Paul Perry*

About the Authors

PAUL PERRY—An author living in the great Southwest, Paul Perry carries on the business of writing surrounded by cacti and the finest Mexican food known to man. He has written seven books and edited several magazines. In 1980 he was editor of *Running* magazine, where he brought in top writers like Hunter S. Thompson and Ken Kesey to cover road races and sporting events around the globe. He went to China on assignment with Ken Kesey to cover Beijing's first international marathon, and then toured that country for a month in a bus provided by the Chinese government.

KEN BABBS, "THE INTREPID TRAVELLER"—"One night before the bus was born, before the bus was even considered, the Intrepid Traveller was born. He rode the bus cross-country and back and slept in it in Mexico when the axle was broken, followed it to Oregon, and now rests comfortably with it in the field."